SECURE TREATMENT OUTCOMES

Secure Treatment Outcomes

THE CARE CAREERS OF VERY DIFFICULT ADOLESCENTS

Roger Bullock
Michael Little
Spencer Millham
Dartington Social Research Unit

Ashgate

Aldershot • Brookfield USA • Singapore • Sydney

Published by
Ashgate Publishing Limited
Gower House
Croft Road
Aldershot
Hants GU11 3HR
England

Ashgate Publishing Company
Old Post Road
Brookfield
Vermont 05036
USA

British Library Cataloguing in Publication Data
Bullock, Roger
  Secure treatment outcomes : the care careers of very
  difficult adolescents. - (Dartington social research series)
  1.Problem children - Institutional care - Great Britain
  2.Teenagers - Institutional care - Great Britain 3.Juvenile
  detention homes - Great Britain 4.Problem children -
  Services for - Great Britain
  I.Title II.Little, Michael, 1958- III.Millham, Spencer
  362.7'32'0941

Library of Congress Catalog Card Number: 98-70908

ISBN 1 84014 498 X (Hbk)
ISBN 1 84014 458 0 (Pbk)

Printed and bound in Great Britain by
Biddles Ltd, Guildford and King's Lynn

Contents

Index of tables and figures

Preface

This book summarises the key findings from a longitudinal study of young people in long stay secure treatment units. The young people were first admitted to the centres in the mid 1980s and have been followed up during their stay and for two years after leaving. The need to wait for the last young person to have left for two years has caused some delay in publication, but this has been offset by the assembling of a data set comprising comprehensive and reliable data on each case.

During the course of the research five papers were published by the Dartington Social Research Unit. These explore issues in greater detail than is possible in the following pages. They are:

The Characteristics of Young People in Youth Treatment Centres;

The Experiences and Careers of Young People Leaving Youth Treatment Centres;

Alternative Care Careers: The Experience of very Difficult Adolescents outside Youth Treatment Centre Provision;

The Experience of YTC Look-alikes Sheltered in other Settings;

The Part Played by Career, Individual Circumstance and Treatment Interventions in the Outcomes of Leavers from Youth Treatment Centres.

This research could not have been completed without the assistance and support of numerous individuals, government and local authority departments, staff and young people in secure units and their families. We would like to thank especially colleagues at the Social Research Unit, Dr. Lumsden Walker who worked with us on the individual assessments and Dr. David Gordon of Bristol University who advised on the data analysis. A huge debt is also due to all who live and work in the units and on their behalf we thank Trev Edwards, Bill Gregory, Masud Hoghughi, Lionel Jackson, Eugene Ostapiuk and Jim Wilkie.

The Home Office, many probation and social services departments were consulted during the course of the study and we are most grateful for all the help received and for the official support of their staff professional associations.

Finally, we wish to acknowledge the enormous assistance and co-operation from the Department of Health which funded the research. Various divisions were involved in the project and on their behalf we would thank Carolyn Davies, Jenny Griffin, Neville Teller, John Parker, Norman Duncan, Tom Luce and Wendy Rose.

There are many others in all of these organisations who could be named but our deepest gratitude must go to the young people who, despite their difficult circumstances, co-operated in every way.

We are deeply grateful to them all.

1 Introduction

This book explores the care careers of very difficult and disturbed adolescents in long-stay secure treatment units. Most children show isolated psychological problems at one time or another and many children might be described as occasionally 'difficult' or 'disturbed' during their upbringing, but in only a few cases do these labels persist sufficiently for them to merit long-term professional help. Only very few of those well-known to mental health, welfare or youth justice agencies will require placement in a secure specialist unit.

Whatever the context, whether it be residential care, child guidance or mainstream school, adjectives such as 'difficult' and 'disturbed' tend to be freely and widely used. A boy with moderate learning difficulties, a history of epilepsy, looked after away from home and recovering from his fourth placement breakdown is certainly 'difficult', both to manage and to encourage but his problems are not sufficiently severe for him to be included in this study. In the book, *Lost in Care* (Millham et al, 1986), we described the experiences of Gloria, who, by 17 years of age had lived in 25 child care and probation placements. She, too, was undoubtedly 'difficult' and one psychologist diagnosed disturbance, but she was never locked up and a niche in a specialised treatment centre was never entertained. So, what qualities are deserving of the epithets 'extremely difficult and disturbed'?

The adolescents discussed in this study clearly have severe and sometimes chronic problems, usually manifested as some form of conduct or mixed emotional and conduct disorder. However, these are only one part of the equation used to assess eligibility for placement in a secure unit. Quite as important is the professional, administrative and legal frameworks in which the young person's problems are addressed. Many are too immature to be safely placed in prison department

1

custody, although their offending behaviour may make such a placement a legal possibility. Some of those scrutinised in the coming pages display bizarre behaviour patterns, such as killing the family pets, but, despite undergoing numerous assessments, are not found to be mentally ill - at least in the formal sense of displaying disorders of thought, speech or perception - consequently they are not viewed as suitable for hospital treatment. A salient feature of young people who become candidates for long-term security is their tendency to present problems which cannot be effectively met by a single agency or intervention. Frequently, the result is an eclectic approach which attempts to incorporate the best features of several specialisms.

The failure to secure a clear label, such as mental illness, does not signal tranquillity. Not only do the young people in question pose a danger to the public, they also put themselves at risk. Their pathology is complex, frequently involving unusual family circumstances and social relationships. Looking back from the day of entry to a specialised treatment centre, the influence of risk factors such as poor family functioning appear obvious. Yet looking forward reveals a multitude of young people with exactly the same risk factors who never got into any trouble.

Not surprisingly, therefore, the subjects of this book attract attention out of proportion to their number, often elbowing aside concern for larger groups of other troubled and troublesome adolescents. When placed in prison custody, those studied here mesmerise prison officers, causing greater anxiety than the persistent property offenders who crowd the cells of young offender institutions. Similarly, in child care contexts, this minority group of disordered, acting out adolescents can shatter the confidence of staff who might have achieved reasonable gains with the less difficult.

As we shall see, in order to be included in this study, adolescents have to have exhausted the best of social services, health and education placements. As a consequence, transfer to secure accommodation was deemed essential and a short-stay was unlikely to be sufficient. Most civilised societies guard against the danger of locking up young people too readily or of making placements simply on the basis of the resources available rather than according to the child's needs but for these young people even the most fervent children's rights campaigner would concede the need for custody. But, as well as the requirement to hold onto these adolescents and to protect both them and the public, some form of 'help' with their problems is a necessity. As will be seen, extended periods of 'treatment' are a common experience.

Although the study says much about those difficult and disturbed adolescents who cause concern in all economically developed nations, in England certain groups have been specifically omitted. Those formally diagnosed as mentally ill have been excluded (although North American readers will note that this category does not include those with a conduct or mixed conduct and emotional disorder). Also left out are those who are difficult to place but who do not need extended stays in secure treatment settings; neither does the persistent property offender found within the youth custody system find a niche, even though many of the young people described exhibit some of their characteristics. What is left is a relatively small group of very difficult adolescents, who number around 150 in England and Wales at any one time. These are the focus of this book.

Problems presented by very difficult young people

Most economically developed nations are faced with problems resulting from the behaviour of young people. While many adolescents display casual and irreverent attitudes to societal constraints, they do not get into serious trouble. Indeed, the National Child Development Study found that less than 900 in 10,000 young people ever come to the notice of juvenile justice agencies, with 300 getting special education services. But the minority placed away from their families can pose difficulty for those responsible for their care, particularly when they run away, are violent, threaten their carers or when past behaviour intimates future risk, such as those young people convicted of grave crimes.

In setting up the research for this book, each of these categories loomed. Most common were those young people who repeatedly fail to settle in the best open care situations available to health, education and social services. As they are adolescents, residential services were tried with great frequency, although specialised foster placements played a part. 'Best care situations' are those that display the features shown by research as likely to promote children's welfare and to facilitate normal development. Several studies from Dartington and elsewhere demonstrate that good results are more likely if children feel enriched by their care experience.

Although good care was on offer, the young people in this study failed to benefit. In many cases, they persistently ran away, putting themselves or others at risk. But running away, though a nuisance and occasionally dangerous, is not in itself a sufficient condition for a long stay in a secure treatment setting; indeed, flight from some care settings might be considered a sign of adjustment. But persistent disruption within and running away from benign open conditions often result in a downward spiral of lack-lustre, temporary, crisis driven palliatives, a rake's progress that exacerbates children's problems.

Violent adolescents also generate concern but, again, such behaviour need not imply long spells of treatment. Specialised interventions are only required when the aggressive behaviour exhausts all other modifying efforts, possibly springing from disorders of personality as well as the contexts in which young people find themselves. Violent adolescents obviously frighten those looking after them but caution still needs to be exercised when deciding which of this group should be locked-up. Aggression in the young is often situational, precipitated by the actions of others, usually adults. So, restraining violent young people by placing them in secure accommodation can increase as well as decrease tensions. Nonetheless, the unpredictably dangerous child can benefit from containment.

The study also includes young people convicted of grave offences who, *de facto*, need extended periods in a secure setting because of the danger they pose to themselves or to the public or because public opinion is unlikely to tolerate their staying in the open community. But not all these young murderers, rapists or arsonists require treatment interventions; some might mature into healthy adults without the paraphernalia of psychotherapy, behaviour modification or other specialist interventions.

Administrative structures for providing services for difficult adolescents

Many nations have evolved a myriad of services designed to meet the needs of troubled adolescents. Consequently, young people's problems can be dealt with in any one of or a combination of welfare and control systems. For example, in England and Wales it is possible for a serious offender, such as a rapist, to be dealt with by social services, although most are sent by courts to prison. In nearly all European Union States, the violent aggressive child can be sheltered either in custody, education/child-care or mental health provision; in England and Wales the latter has been viewed as a more benign and less stigmatising option, often used by middle-class parents coping with recalcitrant children.

In addition to a choice of services, there are several legal options available for difficult young people. They may be taken into the care of the State, usually under a care order rather than under voluntary arrangements. In England and Wales this remains an option for those convicted of grave crimes such as arson or rape, as well as for the tiny proportion of young people looked after away from home for welfare reasons, who need to be placed in specialist secure accommodation solely because of their difficult behaviour. Such placements have to be ratified by a court. Mental health orders offer another route to security but, although relatively common in the United States, they are rare in England and Wales, but the option exists. Serious offenders can be sentenced by a criminal court to custody, usually in separate young offender institutions, but those convicted of grave crimes can also be sentenced to custody or to detention under mental health laws. In England and Wales, these offenders often elicit a Section 53 disposal (Section 53 of the *Children and Young Persons Act*, 1933). Sub-section one allows children convicted of murder to be detained at 'Her Majesty's pleasure'. Sub-section two allows children to be detained for a period from two years to life when convicted of crimes which, were they adult, would merit long sentences of 14 years or more.

The service and legal options for young people do not always coincide in the way that most observers would expect. For example, because young people sentenced under Section 53 can be placed wherever Her Majesty (or Her representative) sees fit, placement at home (though unlikely) remains a possibility and it was rumoured that one offender was successfully rehabilitated in a private boarding school. Other grave offenders, particularly those long known to social services, may continue to be looked after by the State, while others in prison custody clearly need and may benefit from the specialist help that education, mental health or social services can provide.

Despite such variety in provision and legal options, it remains difficult to help some young people with very unusual needs and adolescents can follow avenues ill suited to their problems. This has led some countries to open specialised centres reserved for 'the most difficult and disturbed'; in England and Wales these take the form of regional secure units run by local authorities and, until recently, two Youth Treatment Centres, Glenthorne and St. Charles.

In Britain, throughout the 1950s and 1960s it was felt that a small number of adolescents, especially girls, were presenting such severe problems that training schools for delinquents, social services or health authorities could not adequately meet their needs. A different residential initiative was required and a new treatment approach was long overdue. There were debates between the Home Office (responsible for both prisons and child care until 1971) and the Health Department (responsible for health and for social services after 1971) about which department should take responsibility for these young people. Health maintained that such adolescents were unlikely to respond to hospital treatment and would seldom merit a diagnosis of 'mental illness', while the Home Office felt that the young people's needs exceeded those which youth custody could reasonably be expected to meet.

The debate, vociferous at the time that new legislation the *Children and Young Persons Act*, 1969 was going through Parliament, coincided with considerable public concern about the tragic case of Mary Bell, a ten year old who murdered two small children but whose needs could not be met by current provision in hospital, prison or social services.

This gave an impetus to the argument for specialised provision, particularly to the development of the Youth Treatment Centres which were designed for such cases. They were to offer long term treatment facilities, with gradations of security for seriously disturbed children and adolescents. The task was to check deterioration in children's anti-social behaviour, to prevent further personality damage and to increase general understanding of severe disturbance among juveniles. By combining the facilities, strength and potential of several established approaches, such as residential care, special education, hospitals and aspects of the borstal system, it was hoped a more therapeutic approach to difficult children could be fashioned. St. Charles Youth Treatment Centre came into being in 1971 and Glenthorne in 1978. Through two turbulent decades they provided 70 secure beds until St. Charles closed in 1995.

Life route, process, career route and the prediction of outcomes

Two dimensions of troubled children's lives have been used by Dartington in successive studies to understand what happens to young people passing through the administrative and legal systems just described. The first is *life route*, that is to say the decisions that a young person (and his or her family) make which affect life chances. To make an accurate prognosis, it is necessary to build up a picture which begins at birth and covers all areas of a child's life. It is evident from previous research that choice in one area, such as living situations, can affect others, say family and social relations. The concept of life route also incorporates the individual's personality as this affects conduct. For very difficult young people, behaviour will reflect pathological conditions, such as conduct, emotional or mixed disorders. Thus, problems of running away, violence and offending which necessitate some form of intervention need to be included.

The second dimension is *process*, defined as the decisions made by professionals and/or courts (in response to the young person's life route) which affect life chances. So, whether an adolescent is picked up by education, child guidance, social or health services will probably make a difference to long-term outcomes. Similarly, a court's preference for a Section 53 sentence rather than youth custody or even a care order is likely to influence the psychological and social development of a troubled adolescent and the way he or she is perceived by others.

Such an approach incorporates the background circumstances, needs and pathology of the young person and his or her family as well as the interventions fashioned to ease difficulties. Getting into trouble with the law - which is one aspect of life route - clearly has an effect on long term life chances but so does the decision of using the youth justice system - part of the *process*. Similarly, while key life events, such as the death of a parent, an accident or sexual abuse, are likely to affect a child's functioning, so can the quality of social and other welfare agencies' response to the problem: it is unlikely, for example, that several placement breakdowns while away in state care and loss of contact with relatives will do much to enhance a young person's life chances or behaviour.

As the reader needs to juggle with many variables contributing to an outcome, it helps if the interaction between the decisions of child and family on the one hand and those of support agencies on the other are subsumed under *career route*. It will be seen in Chapters Six, Seven and Nine that decisions made at successive moments in a career will influence what happens subsequently. For example, an adolescent sentenced to youth custody is highly unlikely subsequently to gain a place in an elite public school - although one or two public school boys have secured a place in young offender institutions. But there are more subtle links; for instance, children in state care or accommodation suffering placement disruption also tend to do badly at school. There is also a link between the unease generated in others by children who murder and the offenders' subsequent social isolation.

Career route - so defined - is a useful way of categorising the situations of children and young people in need. The numerous children referred to welfare and control agencies for help will follow many career routes. Five became evident in the research for this book. Those who interrupted apparently blameless lives with a one-off grave offence are clearly distinguishable from those long known to education and/or social services or those who are both seriously and persistently delinquent. The details of the five career routes emerge in Chapter Four and form the basis for analysing subsequent outcomes.

But career route is more than just classification; its value is in prediction, encouraging us to say within a reasonable margin of error what a troubled adolescent's future life chances will be. Prediction is a notoriously complicated process and, when undertaken for a general population, very difficult. For example, to help identify young people who might need help in the future, a general population of, say, 10,000 children might be screened for a pathology which is known to affect, say, five percent of adolescents. Established risk factors would be used to identify those individuals likely to succumb. If the predictive power of the factors is 80%, then 8,000 predictions will be correct and 2,000 wrong. Of the 500 who actually develop the pathology, 400 will be correctly predicted and 100 incorrectly. This means that a failure rate of 20% wrongly identifies as at risk 1,900 of the 9,500 children not affected. Thus, the value of achieving 400 correct predictions is somewhat reduced by the 1,900 'false positives' unnecessarily entering the screening programme. Such results are likely to be of limited value to practitioners seeking to identify who within the general population will need help in the future.

Prediction in this study, however, is of a different order, since the starting point is the high risk case already known to a welfare or control agency and the prognosis concerns their future life chances. Moreover, while the starting point is the career route to which the young person belongs, the subsequent analysis focuses upon individual adaptations - trying to predict from research knowledge what could best be achieved from the point at which the label 'extremely difficult and disturbed' was applied and, conversely, what is the worst scenario. This, as we shall demonstrate, is likely to be helpful to those wishing to assess future needs and risks.

We try in this study to estimate both the contribution of a young person's personal resources and the treatment intervention to subsequent progress. This is to say that, given the research knowledge about young people's careers, an individual on a particular career route might expect the following experiences over the next two years; but if influences are operating that 'modify, ameliorate or alter a person's response to an environmental hazard' (Rutter's definition of protective factors), outcomes will be better. The effects of the treatment intervention are also measured. The benefit of this approach to the data on the young people scrutinised should become apparent in Chapter Nine.

The important message of this approach is that outcomes are predictable. We shall see that very few of the young people followed up behaved in unexpected ways. This evidence should be heartening to those who work with very difficult adolescents, especially when it is combined with findings on what works, for whom, when and where and with multivariate analysis of factors associated with bad outcomes - as found in Chapter Eight.

The relevance of research into very difficult adolescents

Research evidence about extremely difficult adolescents has not always played a part in the formulation of policy or the development of practice guidelines. As in so much that has been done on behalf of vulnerable children, provision tends to have developed piecemeal without much knowledge about the young people: who they are, what they will respond to and what happens to them as they grow into adulthood. It is a remarkable fact that up to £100,000 per annum per young person can be spent on the most specialised interventions with little, if anything, known about outcomes.

Evaluating interventions for those in greatest need of help also has relevance for those working with more routine cases. Many developments in social work have been achieved because back-up facilities are available for those who strive to keep adolescents out of residential care, secure accommodation or youth custody. If community alternatives are to work, specialist facilities are necessary for the relatively small proportion who fail in such approaches. The messages learnt from these young people also help us understand the processes and factors associated with the need for expensive resources, such as long term secure units. Despite some improvements in practice during the last 30 years, many of the young people described in the coming pages are still casualties of the system and better care and control earlier on might have dispensed with much subsequent turmoil, upset, time and expense.

The findings presented in this book also have implications for child care policy and practice. As the young people's situations partly reflect their responses to our interventions, a change in policy towards troublesome children will produce fluctuations in the number of very difficult adolescents dealt with by means of specialised secure treatment units. If prison was felt to be unhelpful to those under the age of 21 years, the consequence for social services would be considerable, not least because they would find themselves responsible for many extremely difficult clients. On the other hand, if British psychiatrists were to follow their North American colleagues and admit more behaviourally disordered children to hospital, then the burden on social services would ease.

Although the focus of this book is on a small number of extremely difficult and disturbed young people dealt with in long stay secure treatment units, it is hoped that readers will find the material has wider relevance. The coming pages will consider how the young people in question can be identified and what can be done for them.

2 Services for disordered adolescents: defining who is very difficult

The history of institutions reveals a continuous conflict between those who wished to separate youthful offenders from adults and those who did not. The rationale was usually more concerned with contamination than with more liberal approaches and many who sought reform still saw juvenile crime as a reflection of moral turpitude and original sin. Mary Carpenter, for example, objected to Sidney Turner's Parkhurst for young offenders not because it was benign but because it was part of the prison system. Despite some early attempts at diversion, it was not until the late eighteenth and nineteenth centuries that initiatives specific to delinquent children, such as the Marine and the Royal Philanthropic Societies, expanded and not until the mid-nineteenth century that legislation formalised the establishment of distinct services for them, for example following the implementation of the *Reformatory Schools Act* (1854) and the *Industrial Schools Act* of 1857. While delinquent adolescents have long enjoyed their own provision, concerns about their welfare and special needs, as we now perceive them, are more recent.

This chapter describes the processes for dealing with difficult adolescents in England and Wales. The services are different from those in other countries, even from Scotland which tends to be more liberal in its approach or Northern Ireland which tends to be more punitive. But the principles which underpin the provision and the difficulties that have dogged its development are common, at least to North America and the European Union. These overarching themes and perspectives also emerge in the coming pages.

The aim is to discover where extremely difficult and disturbed young people might be found and to establish clear criteria against which candidates for inclusion in this study can be judged. In the following chapters these criteria are applied to adolescents sheltered in several treatment settings in England and Wales. Those deemed worthy of further scrutiny are then examined in greater detail.

Processes for dealing with difficult adolescents in England and Wales

Young people in need are processed along a variety of avenues. Their problems may become manifest in school, requiring special education, child guidance or occasionally mental hospital. Difficulty associated with the family is more likely to result in the State looking after the young person, either on a care order or on a voluntary basis. Offenders are processed through juvenile justice. Those who present the greatest difficulty often cross agency boundaries, such as delinquents placed in local authority accommodation or young people beyond the control of special schools, both these groups can make their way to social services secure settings. A referral reflects both the concern of the agencies involved and the previous life routes taken by children. Naturally, many are called but few are chosen for the most specialised provision in any sector because of constraints on resources.

What happens to those whose difficulty requires some form of physical containment? Following the careers of adolescents in secure settings is complicated by the fact that, although there are clear legislative and administrative procedures for handling such cases, the different statutory authorities - health, social services and Home Office - often share facilities. Thus, within any secure unit run by local authority social services, there will be young people who are the responsibility of several different central and local departments. Older adolescents on remand jostle with convicted offenders and the behaviourally disordered, some of whom will be in state care.

As will be seen, in addition to the legal and administrative categories, there are many informal decisions based on professional discretion which can influence the route taken by a difficult adolescent. A look at the routes taken by young people destined for long-stay secure units and the various by-ways along which some difficult children are diverted to other settings helps clarify the situation.

Although the heterogeneous nature of entrants to such long-stay units is apparent from even the briefest scrutiny of the later chapters, arrivals will have followed one of three legal and administrative avenues already described. As the following diagram illustrates, the high road is taken by children in state care or accommodation who display serious behaviour problems. Some of them, but not all, will have committed offences. The second avenue involves serious offenders, a number of whom also display other behavioural difficulties. A third route, frequently taken by children displaying disturbed behaviour from an early age, is special education and mental health. Not only does the diagram illustrate the different routes that children take but it also shows the relationship between them.

Figure 2.1: Three legal and administrative avenues available for extremely difficult and disturbed children in England and Wales

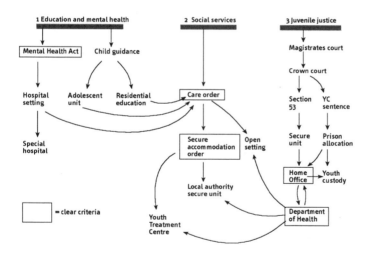

Looking at the three avenues in more detail, it can be seen that many very difficult young people may, if circumstances warrant and parents agree, be accommodated by local authority social services under a voluntary agreement. Alternatively, they may be taken into care if the court is satisfied that the young person is suffering, or is likely to suffer, significant harm and that the harm is attributable to the care previously offered or to his or her being beyond parental control. Should the young person's behaviour continue to deteriorate to the point of needing secure accommodation, the court must decide whether the criteria in Section 25 of the *Children Act*, 1989 have been met. These state that '(i) he (or she) has a history of absconding and is likely to abscond from any other description of accommodation; and (ii) if he (or she) absconds suffering of significant harm is likely; or that if he or she is kept in any other description of accommodation he (or she) is likely to injure him or herself or other persons.'

For these young people, a number of options are available. Initially, placement in local authority secure accommodation, usually for a short period, will be arranged. There are 28 secure units offering 362 beds in England designed for this purpose. Should longer term treatment be entertained, a place might be sought from the Youth Treatment Centre which has 40 beds - requiring that another set of conditions are met. Traditionally, four units in Durham, Lancashire, Leeds and Bristol have provided for longer stays, although no official distinction is made with regard to their status. Naturally, the greater the sophistication of the resource being sought, the greater will be the constraints on social workers' freedom of action; whether a place is available, whether the local authority will meet the cost and whether the secure setting considers they can help the child. All of this stands between the assessment of an adolescent's needs and the placement becoming available.

Many adolescents are young offenders and enter the system via youth justice. Some aged between 15 and 17, because of the persistence or the seriousness of their offending, will be sentenced to youth custody for periods of between two months and two years. Those aged 18-20 may be sentenced to between three weeks and an unlimited period. A minority of young people commit grave offences. As a result, there will first be a hearing in the Magistrates Court and, using another set of guidelines, a decision is made whether or not to pass the case on to the Crown Court. If the child is found guilty in the Crown Court, three disposals are available. First, the judge may sentence the young person to a period of youth custody. Second, it is possible, although unlikely, that the court will be more benign in its disposal and, for instance, give a probation order allowing the young person to remain in the community. Third, the judge can make a Section 53 sentence, under the *Children and Young Persons Act*, 1933 which, as described in the previous chapter, allows an indeterminate period of detention in the case of murder and a fixed period - usually for between two and six years - for lesser crimes.

It is not only the disposal that determines the routes taken by serious offenders. A judge's decision to use the Section 53 option widens the range of placements in which the young person might be sheltered; Youth Treatment Centre or other child-care treatment settings become possible. But the judge's written recommendations also influence decisions made about the young person in future years, not least the duration and place of detention.

The court decision is complemented by a set of formal procedures at the Home Office and Department of Health to determine placement. A horrendous murder by a juvenile will merit his or her case receives careful and constant scrutiny at the highest levels in a way that a less emotive crime might not. But, again, informal mechanisms operate. Some Section 53 cases are sent to prison department allocation centres where the decision to refer to the Department of Health responsible for admission to treatment or child-care establishment rests with senior staff who may have little experience of young offenders or Section 53 sentences, especially as there are less than 200 such sentences passed each year.

The final set of avenues in the preceding diagram come under the heading of education and mental health services. Most young people in this sector are behaviourally disordered rather than mentally ill and nearly all who continue to need help are referred on to the social services avenues. A tiny minority - no national figures are compiled - are diagnosed as mentally ill or have a borderline personality disorder. If the conditions laid out in the *Mental Health Act*, 1983 are met, then a place in a mental hospital will be found. Some of the marginal cases will, on a psychiatrist's recommendation, be transferred to social services avenues and occasionally some slip through into youth custody. The Gardener Unit at Prestwich Hospital, for example, which undertakes observation and assessment, sees 40% of its leavers return home and 60% move on to other secure units.

Observation on the process

As was explained at the beginning of the chapter, the processes just described have evolved in response to particular conditions existing at different moments in the history of services for children and young people in need. The separation of young from adult prisoners led to many initiatives and eventually to the creation of institutions which we today call youth custody. The closure of the reform schools - later known as Approved Schools - in the 1970s increased pressure for local authority secure beds. The absence of provision for the case of Mary Bell, a child convicted of murder, influenced the creation of the Youth Treatment Service. Given a *tabula rasa* on which to design a new service to meet the needs of difficult and disturbed young people, it is likely that the myriad of laws, routes and procedures, to say nothing of the institutions they serve, would be swept away. The complexity of the process contrasts with other parts of child welfare and juvenile justice systems where there is more logic and flexibility.

The overriding feature of available services is its tendency to be provision rather than needs led. If new treatment centres open, their beds fill with the rejects of the three sectors just described. If an institution closes - as has St. Charles Youth Treatment Centre - its catchment population switches seemingly effortlessly into other settings which have entirely different standards - like youth custody. The finding by Stewart and Tutt that in 1984 the North of England had twice the rate of young people in custody or secure accommodation than the South - including London - confirms the provision-led nature of the systems. Among the reasons why the North had twice the rate of young people locked up was because it has twice the rate of secure beds available.

This provision-led aspect of the process is reflected in the marginality of the young people referred. They are not and seldom have been 'clubbable'. Hardly integrated into home, most of the young people have found it difficult to find a niche in education, mental health, juvenile justice or social services. Indeed, the majority have commanded the attention of several agencies and the unfortunate have been shunted from professional to professional, some failing to get the help they clearly require. Thus, although suffering a conduct disorder, the young people who are the focus of this book stand out among the borderline mentally ill in adolescent units. Although in need of custody, the young person will be uncomfortable among other inmates in a young offender institution. Even in specialised treatment centres, the common denominator appears at first glance to be the fact that nobody else wants these residents.

But their marginality within existing services does not mean that the process fails to influence the lives of these young people. Quite the contrary. More than any other young people we have studied, the interventions of statutory agencies have had a discernible effect on the lives of those scrutinised in this book. Many have lived away from home or been subject to specialist interventions for as long as they can remember. Those seemingly unproblematic until late adolescence might be thought of as exceptions to this rule but watching somebody arrested for murder languish in the cell of a young offender institution, trying to make sense of the extraordinary chain of events set in process by the crime of which they are accused, rapidly revises one's opinions.

Marginality is frequently accompanied by notoriety. The grave offenders stand out by virtue of their crime. Murder, arson and rape are comparatively rare crimes and it is rarer still for a young person to be convicted of such an offence. The media can show an interest and occasionally, as in the case of Jamie Bulger, a two year old murdered by two 10 year olds in 1994, the crime attracts international interest and evokes national reflection on the state of society. Even if the press fail to pick on the case, it is highly likely that the local community will. The situation of a youngster from a Turkish family who responded well enough to his treatment programme to be released to the community but could not go home because of the risk of harm from incensed neighbours provides a vivid example, as does the difficulty faced by a violent teenager returning to a small village. Both cases served as reminders of the exceptional nature of the subjects of this study.

Those failing to evoke public scrutiny by virtue of their crimes, often manage it on the basis of the high cost of sheltering them. One local authority, anxious to avoid spending the £2,000 a week needed for a specialised, secure treatment bed, purchased a house on behalf of an extremely damaged youngster in their care and allocated four full time social workers to look after him. The economy drive ended when the young person burned the house down and elected social services committee members reluctantly agreed to fund a Youth Treatment Centre place. Even those in relatively inexpensive prison department settings draw heavily on the public purse by virtue of the length of time they have to be incarcerated.

The fact that the State is prepared to shoulder the burden of such high costs reflects the particularly sensitive nature of the problems being tackled. A single individual can encompass both welfare and justice concerns. There is usually a consensus that the young person should be locked up and, where a crime has been committed, that he or she is seen to be punished. But the offender might be a victim of abuse, neglect or disadvantage him or herself. Moreover, if he or she is very young, immature or has learning difficulties, it can be inappropriate, if not dangerous, to lock him or her up in an institution designed for older young offenders, like youth custody. The response of the State reflects the natural urge to punish and deter others and an equally natural drive to offer young people opportunities for atonement, reform and treatment.

These influences on decision making - often contradictory - are manifest in the apparently haphazard amalgam of processes described in the earlier diagram. For every legal statute, there are several administrative channels to navigate, through Home Office, Department of Health and local and health authorities. For every formal procedure, there are several informal mechanisms bound up in the traditions and practices of prison officers, social workers and mental health professionals. There is even a role in this process for the executive, although the involvement of the Home Secretary in the setting of sentences for Section 53 grave offenders has been subject to criticism and has been reviewed by the European Court of Human Rights, whose judgement may require revision of the 1933 legislation.

None of the observations made in the preceding pages applies exclusively to processes for difficult and disturbed adolescents. The same provision-led features are apparent in child protection services. The mix between legal, formal and administrative procedures can also be seen in services for children looked after away from home. But, as with so much else in this study, each of these features is more marked for very difficult young people. Thus, many of the new ways of thinking about children's services, for example of finding mechanisms to prioritise risk, setting out eligibility for services, ensuring that provision matches the needs of the child and identifying a single process leading to a continuum of interventions, have not been adopted by those working with the most difficult young people in society.

These questions will re-emerge in the concluding pages of this book. For now, it is sufficient to acknowledge that the process - the response of welfare and control agencies to a young person's difficulty - is clearly going to influence long-term life chances. The task for this study has been to distil findings in a way that improves understanding of young people's career routes and to fashion predictive models which can be used by policy makers and professionals to refine and improve what is on offer for these young people. But to be in a position to do this, it is first necessary to know where to look for these adolescents and ask by what criteria they can be selected from others who are difficult but not 'in extremis'.

Resident populations of secure settings in England and Wales

Having described the processes for dealing with these very difficult young people, it is worth taking stock and glancing at the State's endeavour with such adolescents. How many young people under the age of 17 are under lock and key in England and Wales, which has a total population of 55 million and a child population of 11 million? Under what conditions are these young people detained? The following table summarises the situation at the beginning of 1997.

Table 2.1: The number of young people aged under 17 in secure settings on a selected day and admitted to such placements over a year

Prison department	In secure settings on one day	Admitted during the year
Remanded	168	2,090
Convicted	655	2,502
Sub-total	823	4,592
Local Authority/YTCs		
Secure Units	274	829
Youth Treatment Centres	40	20
Sub-total	314	849
Mental Health	50	100
TOTAL	**1,187**	**5,541**

(Prison figures are for 1996, snapshot at 30 June; prison annual admissions are based on age on sentence; local authority figures are for places available on 31 December 1996; figures for mental health are estimates. Some 14% of residents and 3% of admissions to local authority units are aged over 16; these are included in the figures. Prison figures, in contrast, rise some 250% if 17 year olds are included to 2,093 residents and 11,798 annual admissions.)

There were, then, several places to look for the extremely difficult youngsters who were to form the focus of this study. Three sectors, seven types of secure institutions and over 100 places had the potential to shelter these adolescents. The natural place to begin looking were the two Youth Treatment Centres as they were established to cater for the most difficult young people and had the most elaborate gate keeping procedure in the entire system, suggesting that they were a precious facility for adolescents presenting complex problems. However, it is clear from what has been said that promising candidates can miss specialised services and go instead to youth custody. Indeed, in a survey conducted on a particular day in 1987, 351 young people were found serving extended sentences of youth custody or periods of detention under Section 53 of the 1933 *Children and Young Persons Act*. All of these young offenders were considered as potentially extremely difficult and disturbed.

Additionally, it was necessary to look at the populations of local authority secure units. On 31st March 1987, the date when the series of major follow-up studies underpinning this book began, there were 317 children sheltered in such settings, the majority by way of a secure accommodation order but also 44 detained under Section 53 legislation. As has been noted, most secure units are short-term holding centres and very difficult youngsters living in such settings eventually move on to a placement which can offer an extended period of treatment or to detention. As such, the short-term units were excluded from this research. However, within the local authorities' provision there were also the four long-term secure units: Aycliffe in County Durham, Red Bank in Lancashire, East Moor in Leeds and Kingswood (now replaced by Vinney Green) in Bristol, although as was explained, this specialism no longer applies. Together, these four units sheltered 92 children on 31st March 1987. Most of the residents were subject to care and secure accommodation orders but about one-third were detained under Section 53 legislation.

Criteria for inclusion in the study

As the greatest number of gate-keeping procedures - in the form of legislation, administrative structures and informal mechanisms - stood between difficult young people and a place in the most specialised setting, the Youth Treatment Centres, it seemed sensible to use these criteria to identify the study population. Research by Cawson and Martell and later by Dartington showed that many children in secure accommodation, including the Youth Treatment Centres, were inappropriately placed in that they did not actually need the facilities offered. Subsequently, administrative and legislative procedures were tightened. At the time the research began, the Youth Treatment Centres applications panel applied the following criteria when considering whether to offer a place at Glenthorne or St. Charles to a very difficult and/or disturbed child.

Any referral must ensure:

a) that the young person is on an order or sentence which allows placement in security;

b) that the young person is in urgent need of long-term care in secure conditions;

c) that all other forms of intervention have been exhausted or are unsuitable;

d) that the young person is capable of achieving a degree of adjustment;

e) that the local authority or Home Office will be able to ensure that the young person will be able to spend at least 12 months in a specialised treatment setting and will stay in security for as long as is necessary.

In addition to meeting these general criteria for entry, the following features of young people's backgrounds were considered before making a final decision as to their suitability for a specialised treatment place:

f) that the young person is aged under 17½ years or, if older, is manifestly unsuitable for placement in an adult institution;

g) that the young person qualifies for placement in secure accommodation because of persistent absconding, violence or danger to self or others;

h) that, if not a grave offender, the young person has experienced at least two placement breakdowns in open conditions which offered care of the highest quality;

i) that psychiatric assessment has ruled out formal mental illness in terms of distortions of speech, thought or perception, but has diagnosed a conduct or mixed disorder viewed as likely to be amenable to treatment.

In the next chapter, it will be seen that at any one time in England and Wales there are between 110 and 150 young people meeting these criteria.

Conclusion

This chapter has described the complex process by which difficult and disturbed young people are dealt with in England and Wales. It has shown three main avenues that can be followed by difficult and disturbed young people, starting with social services, education or youth justice but leading to considerable overlap as young people's problems increase. The details of the legal statutes, administration and informal decision making involved will differ from that in place in other European or North American countries, but the underlying principles and the issues which emerge in relation to the most problematic adolescents are much the same across most of the western world. The process described contrasts with recent changes in most public sector agencies which have attempted to develop services that are more needs-led and interventions which are shown by research to achieve optimal outcomes for the young people referred to them. The marginality, notoriety and high public scrutiny of the young people make them rather distinct.

This chapter has also established the criteria by which the most deserving of specialised treatment interventions have been selected from the multitude of adolescents who cause themselves, their parents and, less frequently, the State concern. In the next Chapter, the whereabouts of these extremely difficult cases are traced and a way of exploring the characteristics of the young people, their response to different types of intervention and those factors which best explain their long-term outcomes is laid out.

3 Selecting the cases and designing the study

The criteria for inclusion in this study comprise a mixture of legal orders, factors indicating the degree of difficulty presented by the young person and an estimation of their ability to respond to treatment. They reflect a pre-occupation with the young person's conduct - as defined in the opening chapter - and the processes in place to deal with it. By definition, some extremely difficult and disturbed young people have been excluded from the study. Those diagnosed as seriously mentally ill are a significant omission. Although they number only a few per thousand of the adolescent population in England and Wales, such young people draw heavily upon specialist services; yet little is known about their long-term situations. Nonetheless, their circumstances are sufficiently distinct from the young people described in this study to warrant their exclusion.

The initial analysis also identified where to look for possible candidates for the investigation. The destinations of the avenues on the process map on page 13 seemed most likely to reap dividends. So, we scrutinised the Youth Treatment Service of the Department of Health, the four long-term secure units operated by the local authorities, young offender institutions administered by the Home Office and adolescent units in mental health.

Progress was hindered by the different proportions of young people meeting the criteria in each of the institutions visited. At first glance, all of the residents in the Youth Treatment Centres seemed to meet the criteria, an encouraging finding given the results of Cawson and Martell's study a decade earlier when many under lock and key did not. However, successive snapshot surveys of residents in young offender institutions failed to identify any inmates who qualified as extremely difficult and disturbed although it was known that some, such as those convicted of grave crimes, were to be found in some of these establishments. It was evident that no single method would be sufficient to answer the question of how many candidates for inclusion in this research could be found in the different facilities around the country. So, what was done?

For the Youth Treatment Service, all leavers from two centres over a two year period were considered, 102 young people in total. Not surprisingly all of these cases were found to be candidates for inclusion in that they met most of the criteria.

The long-term secure units required another strategy. All four were visited to gather information on the characteristics of their residents, their admission criteria and their treatment approaches. Data was sufficiently reliable to estimate those leavers who met the criteria set out at the end of the last chapter, producing another 135 candidates who had left the units in the same two years as the Youth Treatment Centre graduates and met at least four of the criteria previously described.

The young offender institutions required a very different strategy. Initially, the survey was restricted to those young offenders who had been sentenced to three or more years detention. From an index of 80,000 prison department files, all young people so sentenced and leaving penal institutions over the same two year period as with our other leavers were then considered. This survey produced 88 young people who might be considered candidates for inclusion in the study in the sense that they met at least four of the criteria described on page 21.

Next, mental health avenues were explored. Residents at a regional health authority observation and assessment centre were considered but all candidates subsequently moved on to Youth Treatment Centres, long-term secure units or young offender institutions, findings that have subsequently been confirmed by Bailey and colleagues' (1991) work at the Gardener Unit, Prestwich. Discussions with staff and examination of the files at the John Clare and Mental Handicap Units at St. Andrews Psychiatric Hospital revealed that the majority of their residents were mentally ill. A handful might have been candidates for inclusion in this study but the low number did not warrant a detailed survey.

Finally, the work of the Youth Treatment Centres had shown that about one in 10 of the local authorities in England, Wales and Scotland had never made a referral during the first 15 years of the centres' existence. Some of these authorities made serious claims for community based interventions for difficult young people. However, while these alternatives to secure accommodation and custody were often impressive, when the careers of young people in these localities were carefully monitored, most of the candidates for inclusion in this study ended up in young offender institutions, often rejected by exhausted care workers.

The detailed results of this elaborate exploration have been reported in two papers (Bullock, Little and Millham, 1989 and 1991) but for the purpose of this book, the results can be summarised in the following table which shows that, although there are many difficult young people in the settings surveyed, there are few who can be considered as extremely difficult in terms of this study.

Table 3.1: The number of candidates qualifying for inclusion in the study by the type of placement (numbers based on leavers over a two year period)

	Number of leavers meeting all criteria*	Number of leavers meeting four or more criteria*
Youth Treatment Centre	102	102
Long-term Secure Units	135	11
Young Offender Institutions	88	4
Mental Health Facilities	5	0

* This refers to the criteria laid out on page 21.

This analysis revealed that at the time of the survey there were over 300 young people in the United Kingdom who met at least four of the criteria for inclusion in this study as described in the preceding chapter. The problems posed by these adolescents should not be underestimated. Many were persistent offenders who had been taken into residential care while young and had exhausted most other options including youth custody. Others displayed some characteristics similar to the most difficult cases but their pathology was less severe and therefore aroused slightly less professional concern.

But only 117 of the 330 cases considered met all of the criteria and half of these young people were resident in the two Youth Treatment Centres. However, since one of these centres has closed, it must be assumed that more are now placed in other long term secure units or young offender institutions. By applying the findings nationally, it is estimated that on any one day there are between 110 and 150 young people of the type studied in this book. It may help to know that

England, Wales and Scotland has a population of 55 million with an adolescent (12 - 17) population of 2.5 million. As the table in Chapter Eleven illustrates, the actual number fluctuates according to changes in the adolescent population.

Designing the study

In getting this far, the study had already looked at the files of 330 young people. The simplest method of proceeding would have been to follow-up the 117 leavers who met the criteria for inclusion in the study. Although this figure comprises young people who had been in security for different lengths of time, at least it would offer some knowledge of their outcomes. But, there were also other constraints operating. The research was undertaken at a time when little was known about the circumstances of the very difficult adolescents or the value of sophisticated treatment programmes fashioned to meet their needs. Some of the interventions, like the Youth Treatment Service, were expensive and rapid and encouraging results were required to justify the outlay. To achieve this end, a simple follow-up of leavers would, indeed suffice.

But simple follow-ups are fraught with difficulties of interpretation. This is particularly true of retrospective scrutinies which find patterns and reasons in looking backwards, which were not apparent at the time. If any attempt at explanation is to be successful, some form of prospective analysis, following the young people forward without knowing what will happen, would be required. Naturally, this analysis takes much longer, especially when the time spent in the institution is considerable. One of the sample groups used for the study comprised 56 young people entering the two Youth Treatment Centres in 1986 and 1987. In some cases it was five years before they departed, requiring another two years wait before the follow-up was complete. Longitudinal information takes time to assemble.

Nevertheless, the final research design comprised several complementary approaches which yielded both swift information on what happened to the young people as well as reliable information assembled over a longer time explaining why some young people did better than others. The approach made it possible to answer four questions about extremely difficult and disturbed young people and the services they are offered. These were:

- What is the background and characteristics of extremely difficult and disturbed young people?
- What happens to them in different forms of secure treatment settings?
- What happens to them on leaving these settings?
- Why do some young people do better than others and are some treatment interventions more effective than others?

Background characteristics of the young people

Given that, at the time the fieldwork commenced, the majority of the young people were in the Youth Treatment Centres, it made sense to begin the research with a scrutiny of the characteristics of their residents. Initially, 102 who had left the centres over a two year period were selected. The scrutiny extended to all areas of the young person's life and extended from birth to the point of entry. Information was collected from files, from interviews with the relevant professionals and, only where absolutely necessary, from the young person and his or her family members. The researchers were aided in the data collection and its interpretation by a consultant psychiatrist.

These data were then analysed along the dimension of life route and process described in Chapter One. From this, the dominant career routes in the Youth Treatment Centres emerged, five in all. As the career routes had initially been identified by qualitative work, further analysis was undertaken using quantitative techniques of cluster and discriminant analysis. It was further possible to test the robustness of these groupings on prospective data gathered on another 56 entrants and 46 young people who left the centres in subsequent years. For the sake of clarity, the findings are presented on all 204 young people in the following chapters.

What happens in secure treatment centres?

Much of the work in this area took the form of non-participant observation. The study involved visits to the two Youth Treatment Centres, all four long-term secure units, seven young offender institutions and four mental health facilities. The fieldwork in other areas of work often necessitated stays of several weeks during which time it was possible to piece together exactly what it was the various centres were trying to do for their residents and what was being achieved. Such insights were valuable because, despite the considerable costs attached to these placements, it is seldom thought necessary to write down the nature of the task being undertaken.

In the Youth Treatment Centres, it was possible to take this analysis further by exploring in some depth the work undertaken with residents and analysing the extent to which different strategies yielded positive results. The intention is not so much to set out the finer points of theory about treatment intentions, whether they be psycho-analytic or of other origin, but to specify in simple terms what can be done to help extremely difficult and disturbed youngsters and suggest how interventions can best be matched to the particular needs of young people.

What happens to leavers from secure treatment settings?

On each of the 204 young people studied, information on the background characteristics was gathered and the young people were then followed up for at least two years. Some have been pursued even further into adulthood. In 102 cases, the data collected was retrospective in the sense that respondents were asked to look back over the young person's life. In the other 102 cases, information was carefully checked as it accumulated as the follow-ups were prospective, looking at what happened to the leavers from one month to the next. There are no gaps in this data set. The great benefit to researchers of a study of extremely difficult and disturbed young people is that the cases remain extremely memorable to all who encounter them. The result was a knowledge of the young people that was frequently better than official records, for example, those kept by social workers, probation officers, Home Office or criminal records.

Progress was monitored in all areas of the young person's life. This included living situations, family and social relations, education and employment, physical and psychological health, social and anti-social behaviour and dependency on services. There were complications to overcome in this analysis. For example, some of the leavers from specialist centres move straight on to prison custody. The fact that few of those moving from one secure setting to another re-offend could not be taken as a sign of success. For this reason there have been several re-adjustments to the sample sizes to ensure the correct interpretation of results.

Later on in the study, the question is asked 'did those placed in other settings such as the long-term secure units or young offender institutions fare any better than those going to Youth Treatment Centres?' A similar retrospective study to that just described was mounted on the young people who met the criteria for entry to the Centres but were placed in other establishments.

Why do some children do better than others?

The first study, the retrospective follow-up of 102 Youth Treatment Centre leavers, identified several different career routes of extremely difficult and disturbed young people. It also charted the progress of children in each group, identifying strengths in some areas of the young person's life, such as family and social relationships, and weaknesses in others. For the research to have any value, however, it was necessary to explain rather than just describe these outcomes. Why was it that some of those convicted of a grave crime responded well to treatment and subsequently settled in the community while others languished long in prison often segregated from other inmates? How was it possible for those long known to special education services to achieve more stability in adult life than those who had been long in state care?

To answer these questions, the findings of the retrospective follow-ups were reviewed to discover for each of the career route groups and in each of the six areas of the young person's life what was likely to happen to the young person at best and at worst. So, for those whose offending had been serious and persistent, it was possible to identify where, at best, the young person would be living several years after entering specialist treatment centres, how stable that accommodation would be and with whom he or she would be living. The negative scenario was also set out. This process was repeated for the other four career route groups and then repeated for each of the other areas - family and social relationships; social and anti-social behaviour; education and employment; physical and psychological health; and dependency on state services. The range of possibilities uncovered are described in the Appendix.

This template was then used for the 102 young people who were studied prospectively after leaving the treatment centres. For each, the scenario for the relevant career groups was adapted to account for individual peculiarities. The researchers were helped in this process by a consultant psychiatrist who made independent predictions about the young person's life chances, observations that proved extremely insightful. For example, it was noted that one leaver's mother had long-standing employment as an assistant to a warden of a Cambridge college. The researchers failed to appreciate the risks noted by the clinician that mother's experience of aspirant, good mannered college students might not bode well when coping with the return of her adolescent son graduating from a Youth Treatment Centre. Unable to find work and discouraged by his mother's frequently expressed disappointment, this young man drifted into a drug sub-culture and increasingly unstable living situations, despite many auspicious factors at the point of departure.

The prognoses were made 'blind' at the point of entering the treatment centre. Thus, there was no possibility of knowing what would happen to the young people. The follow-ups then revealed whether these predictions were proved correct and, particularly important, the amount of progress achieved by the young person during their stay in the centres and during the period up to two years after leaving. It was then possible to explore why certain cases did better or worse than was expected from the findings of the retrospective study. Two explanations were explored. First, that the young person made some adaptations not identified at the point of prognosis, which brought some added protection or created additional risk. Second, that the treatment intervention made a difference to long-term outcome.

The results of this work were then used to inform multi-variable analysis of outcomes for all 204 young people leaving specialised treatment centres. Four were selected; first, whether or not the young person offended in the two years since leaving; second, whether he or she was convicted of a serious offence; third, whether there was some rapprochement in family relationships; and, finally, if the young person could be considered to be well adjusted when judged against wider social norms at the two year point.

Conclusion

This chapter has described how the young people were selected for the study and the research methods employed. Application of the selection criteria to populations leaving long-term secure units and young offender institutions over a 2 year period identified 117 young people who met all the conditions. One hundred and two were in the Youth Treatment Centres and 15 elsewhere. When the qualification was dropped to meeting four of the criteria, the number elsewhere rose to 228.

It was decided, therefore, to focus initially on the residents of the two Youth Treatment Centres, leaving comparisons with 'look alikes' until later. Two studies were undertaken: the first was a retrospective scrutiny of all young people who had left the centres over a 24 month period (from a point two years after leaving). The second was a prospective follow-up of all entrants (56) and leavers (46) over a different two year period, also up to a point 24 months after departure. Both samples contained 102 young people, making 204 in all. The follow-up study recorded information from several sources on six aspects of young people's lives: living situations; family and social relationships; social and anti-social behaviour; physical and psychological health; employment and education and dependency on services.

These three data sets (the Youth Treatment Centre leavers studied retrospectively and prospectively and those 'look alikes' placed elsewhere) inform the rest of this book. In the next chapter, young people's background characteristics are analysed and career groups identified. The outcome data on the young people is then used to establish what happens to leavers in each of the career routes in terms of their living situations, family relationships, education and employment (Chapter Six) and their social and anti-social behaviour (Chapter Seven). Thereafter, evidence on careers and outcomes is used to see whether it is possible to predict outcomes either for groups (Chapter Eight) or for individuals (Chapter Nine) and how far the results can be explained in terms of the factors scrutinised in the research (Chapter Ten). Finally, in Chapter Eleven the follow-up results for the young people placed elsewhere are discussed.

One of the golden rules of research is to use sample groups easily explicable to the reader. This maxim has not been achieved in this study. The competing demands for swift descriptive material as well as reliable results have led to a complicated mix of data from different sources. Moreover, in subsequent chapters, the sample size shifts depending upon the question being answered. Nonetheless, it is hoped that the approach succeeds in linking retrospective and prospective data and different types of predictive information. These observations should be borne in mind as the findings of this variety of endeavours are described, beginning in the next chapter with the characteristics of young people.

4 The characteristics of very difficult young people

The previous chapter concluded that the greatest concentration of extremely difficult and disturbed young people at the time this study began were in the two Youth Treatment Centres, Glenthorne and St Charles. The results from the two sample groups previously described, one retrospective designed to set the scene and one prospective intended to explain and predict, are combined for the purposes of this chapter. Together, they supply extensive and reliable information on the characteristics of 204 of the most problematic adolescents in England and Wales. All met the criteria for inclusion in this study as set out in Chapter Two.

The information presented in this chapter was gathered from a variety of sources: from Centre files, from Centre staff and from local authority social workers and probation officers who were interviewed regularly during the follow-up studies. Where necessary to clarify or to complete missing evidence, the young people were interviewed as were their parents, siblings and other relatives or professionals. Evidence from police and criminal records and special secure psychiatric hospital registers was also collated.

Initially, cases were separated into young men and women and then again into those sentenced as grave offenders and those in state care. Because of the complexity of young people's situations, these distinctions later prove to be somewhat unhelpful but they serve to show how the analysis built up.

Table 4.1: Gender and legal status of those in secure treatment settings

| | | Legal Status | |
	State Care	Grave Offender	Total
Male	81	74	155
Female	40	9	49
TOTAL	121	83	204

Gender, age, ethnic group and social class

Of the 204 young people scrutinised, young men outnumbered women by three to one, a ratio which rises to over eight to one for grave offenders. This preponderance of males is at first surprising since it was a lack of treatment facilities for adolescent women that fuelled proposals to establish Youth Treatment Centres. Indeed, the gender ratio is much changed from earlier years; Cawson and Martell found 17 women among the first 32 admissions to St. Charles.

This is not the place to agonise over definitions of race and ethnicity. For simplicity, the ethnicity of the young people is based on their own description of themselves. Excluding those from an Irish background, there were 44 from a minority ethnic group, twice as many as would be expected from the population of England and Wales but a similar proportion to that found among children in state care or custody.

Table 4.2: Ethnicity of young people in specialised treatment centres by legal status

| | Legal Status | |
	State Care	Grave Offender
Afro Caribbean	10	10
Afro Caribbean/White	2	4
Afro Caribbean/Asian	2	0
African/English	2	0
Asian (Sikh)	0	1
Asian	2	3
Asian-English	2	3
Turkish	2	1
TOTAL	22	22

Determining the social class of young people in specialised treatment centres is no easier than defining their ethnicity. There is a high incidence of dislocated families and parents whose class affiliations are in flux. As would be expected, the majority of those in state care and accommodation were from poor working class families. Nonetheless, a fifth of all those studied came from broadly middle-class families; a proportion that is lower than expected when compared with the general population but higher than that for those in State care or custody. Twenty came from homes that were, at least on the surface, both respectable and intact. These were all serious offenders.

The mean age on entry to specialised treatment centres was 15.7 years for young men and 15.9 years for women (with a standard deviation of 1.4 years for both). The average length of stay was just over two years although some stayed much shorter, others much longer (the standard deviation was a year). Young women stayed as long as men. Those on indeterminate criminal sentences following convictions for grave crimes stayed longer (mean=2.7 years) than those on fixed sentences (mean=2.0 years) and those in state care (mean=2.1 years). By the time they left, most leavers were well over 17 years of age.

Social and anti-social behaviour

For most young people, the principal reason for admission to a specialist centre was a behaviour that was either intolerably disruptive and anti-social or which presented a danger to the young person him or herself or to the general public. Many were extremely dangerous. A fifth of those in state care had committed serious offences, indeed 27% of the young men on care orders were admitted to security primarily for this reason. Some of those convicted of grave crimes had been convicted several times for less serious crimes, such as theft and burglary. Some had also already lived in child care and education establishments. When other anti-social behaviours displayed by the young people are scrutinised in detail, a plethora of problems which include delinquency, disruptive behaviour, aggression, running away and sexual difficulties emerged.

A focus on one particular behaviour, offending, in greater detail, reveals a range of patterns both in terms of the seriousness and frequency of delinquency. Eighty three young people, all but nine of them male, were sentenced for grave crimes such as murder and arson to detention under Section 53 of the *Children and Young Person's Act*, 1933. Eighteen were detained 'at Her Majesty's Pleasure', while the remainder were serving fixed-terms, ranging from two to six years for crimes such as assault, aggravated burglary, rape and arson.

The offending behaviour of entrants who had been long in care, accommodation or special residential education, were more difficult to interpret. Petty theft, criminal damage to the fabric of a residential home and assaults on staff are not always followed by prosecution. This was particularly the case for those with emotional and behavioural difficulties who had been long looked after away from home because of neglect or family disruption. For them, petty delinquency in early adolescence rarely led to prosecution or court appearances, making the age of first conviction abnormally high. Others convicted were sometimes dealt with leniently by the courts in an attempt to maintain an existing legal status or care placement.

Bearing these problems in mind, it is more fruitful to examine the persistence of delinquency - which is a strong predictor of future criminal activity - as well as the seriousness of the offences committed. On entry to treatment, 43% had been convicted in court on three or more separate occasions, defining them as persistent delinquents. On many criteria these young people are at high risk of a poor outcome.

To test the seriousness of offending an eight-fold taxonomy was developed. Previous researchers, notably Wadsworth, Bottoms and McClintock will recognise the model. It takes account of whether or not there was a victim involved; whether any property was stolen or damaged and the value of that property; whether the victim suffered physical injury or was placed at serious risk; whether or not the offender was driven by the need for money; and whether or not there was any sexual motive.

The final model is not a rank order of gravity, for although murder is clearly more serious than any other, it would be contentious to state that all property offences have less impact than violent crime. Nonetheless, it does give a better indication of the seriousness of the offence than would a simple description of the crime for which young people are convicted or the severity of the sentences magistrates and judges impose upon them. The following results were obtained from its application:

1. Any crime which leads to loss of life (8%)
2. Violent crime with a sexual motive; e.g. rape, indecent assault (20%)

3. Violent crime in which the offender has no financial motive; e.g. actual or grievous bodily harm (17%)

4. Property offences which involve personal injury to the victim or an assault on the police; e.g. aggravated robbery, resisting arrest or assault (9%)

5. Offences which do not result in personal injury but which place individuals at serious risk and/or lead to considerable financial loss for the victim; e.g. arson (16%)

6. Offences which involve loss and/or damage to property but no personal injury to the victim; e.g. criminal damage/burglary (20%)

7. Offences which involve loss of property but no personal injury; e.g. receiving stolen property (1%)

8. Minor offences which are victimless and non-acquisitive; e.g. speeding (zero)

It will be noted that the above categories only account for 90% of the 204 young people. The remaining 10% had never been convicted before coming to a specialised treatment centre.

Family circumstances and living situations

Difficult behaviour cannot be viewed in isolation from other aspects of the lives and experiences of these young people. One common feature was the unenviable combination of disruption both at home and away from home. Nevertheless, it was surprising that as many as three-fifths (58%) had lived with their families in the year prior to their being placed in a treatment centre and it was at home that the crisis that eventually precipitated them into long-term security first occurred. In some cases, this reflected a 'last effort' to keep the family intact.

Quite a different picture was obtained by looking just at the living situation immediately prior to admission. Only one young person went straight to a treatment centre from home. Nearly half (45%) were already locked up, a third of these being in local authority secure units and two-thirds in youth custody, often on remand. The remainder lived in open establishments, some of which had closed facilities on site.

By the time they arrived at the specialist treatment centre, young people's behaviour problems were well entrenched and they came with long or distinctive experience of residential and secure accommodation. Previous placements had frequently been short, most lasting only a few months. The picture that emerged for those in state care was one of a sequence of substitute placements of diminishing length and increasing restriction.

Compared with some other adolescents long looked after away from home, however, the young people were relatively advantaged in terms of their family structures; most had a number of living relatives and some kind of home-base, even though at the time of entry to the treatment centres, only a quarter (28%) of the young people's families had the natural mother and father living together. Indeed, only 9% had no home or were totally bereft of family support; a figure that is considerably less than for all adolescents in state care. On the other hand, family tensions, exacerbated by the behaviour of the young people themselves, meant that as many as a third (31%) could not return to live with their families, at least for the foreseeable future. As had been expected, the relationships within the families of these adolescents were tense and problematic. The following table summarises young people's home situations at the point of their admission to specialised centres.

Table 4.3: Recent stress factors at home for the 185 young people with a 'home base' (category not mutually exclusive)

	%		%
Frequent membership changes	15	Drink/drugs problem	15
Homelessness	9	Criminality	18
Chronic unemployment	21	Abuse/neglect of children	24
Poor housing	18	Member's physical disability	4
Severe financial problems	31	Member's mental disability	5
Single parenting	42	Family conflicts	61
Member's physical illness	12	Step-parenting	38
Member's mental illness	15		N=185

Although stress factors in the family home were far higher than for the general population, no single feature applied to the majority of admissions. This has been a common finding of studies of troubled adolescents. As Rutter has suggested, it is the summation, sequence and interaction of stress factors that are likely to bring about harm, rather than any particular characteristic. Some stress factors appear much less frequently than might be expected for a high risk group. While, quite naturally, family tensions were common among grave offenders, only a minority had also been neglected or abused or came from families with financial or mental health problems. Cases of homelessness, chronic physical illness, mental and physical disability and drug or alcohol abuse were also relatively uncommon.

The most frequently recorded stress factor in the young person's home was family conflict where relationships were less than tranquil. A third (31%) of the young people had been physically destructive in the family home and a fifth (21%) had frequently run away. Psychiatric assessments indicated that two-fifths (41%) of parents had been over-protective while indifference (18%), intolerance (23%) and outright rejection (15%) also featured. But it was the 'over-protective' group that stood out. Many refused to acknowledge their child's problem or blamed difficulties on external causes. Many of these families had contained problems until the last possible moment. The sudden emergence of difficulties at home, school and in the community reflected a disintegration of this protective shield. All but six of the 84 who had been over protected were male.

Physical and psychological health

Whatever the manifestation of their disturbance, all the young people had behaviour problems and difficulties amenable to treatment, in that their troubles stemmed from early family experiences or subsequent responses to anxiety and stress. Almost all psychiatric and psychological reports confirmed the absence of any formal mental illness in terms of distortions of thought, speech and perception and reached a diagnosis of 'personality' or 'conduct disorder'.

The diagnosis, however, often also referred to mood disorders, such as anxiety or depression, and a few assessments raised the possibility of brain damage syndrome or incipient mental illness. Thus, the majority (55%) of the young people had conditions which crossed Rutter's categories of 'emotional' disorders, such as anxiety and depression, which are often temporary and have a good prognosis, and 'conduct' disorders, such as aggressive or destructive behaviours, which are long-standing and more intractable.

Generally, the placement recommendation sought in psychiatric assessments was for a residential institution which could exert control but also provide a treatment ambience for personal growth, along with educational provision and a social skills programme. Health professionals were requesting an enriching experience that would boost children's self-confidence and reduce anxiety. Naturally, many reports were carefully fashioned to support a referral to a long stay unit, but the consistency of recommendations from several independent sources over several years and requests for help that had clearly remained unmet stood out in the documentation.

Although the previous analysis of presenting behaviours uncovered a varied picture, the psychiatric assessments coalesced to produce an image of a young person from a tense, uncomfortable and sometimes problematic family, having poor interaction skills, both with peers and adults, who was also immature, anxious, emotionally volatile and with a poor self-image. These problems were generally seen as amenable to treatment and were rarely confounded by other major problems of physical or mental health identified in routine checks.

Educational needs

As many of the young people had experienced short placements in a variety of residential settings, their education had been fragmented and stop-gap. Frequent movements and the consequent disruptions to academic courses had long since destroyed the educational ambition of the majority. Indeed, the young persons' educational needs had rarely been paramount when choosing a placement and had usually been attendant on options determined by psychological and other welfare needs.

Moreover, those who had been long in residential care had been offered the limited *curricula* of community homes and secure units described in *Locking Up Children*. It is noticeable in reading educational reports on young people how scant is the mention of achievements in arts, sciences, religion and sport and how rare were opportunities to learn about their cultural heritage and participate in social service, all subjects that would be part of their experience in a good secondary school. Had Caravaggio been alive today he would almost certainly have been placed in care or accommodation and never have seen a paintbrush or canvas.

Even elaborate referral papers failed to give education the salience it deserved. There was almost a sense of hopelessness and irrelevance in the ritual application of I.Q. and reading age tests. Schooling was rarely presented as integral to the treatment plan, despite its possible contribution to social skills training, work experience, self-esteem and integration into the community. However, given its resources, a long-stay treatment centre should be in a strong position to remedy educational deficiencies, even when residents are past the minimum school leaving age.

There was a spread of academic ability among the 204 young people studied; a third (31%) were described as being of low intelligence and a fifth (21%) were assessed as displaying borderline learning difficulties. The majority, in contrast, were of average ability but had poor attainments. For example, 56% had seriously failed to fulfil their academic potential. Very few had had an ordinary schooling; over a third (36%) had attended school irregularly and nearly half (46%) had been expelled at some time, a figure that is particularly high (62%) for those in state care. Consequently, educational disadvantage for some was extreme; 12 (6%) were said to have little knowledge of the outside world, 22 (11%) had very limited ability to help themselves in terms of dress, washing and basic functioning and 23 (11%) were seen as unlikely to survive outside an institution. The study group included a few who could not tell the time or handle money.

Thus, on every dimension selected, young people entering long stay secure treatment centres presented a depressing picture of adolescents gravely limited in their life chances. In terms of family background, personality problems, social skills and educational attainments, their disadvantages were clear. While adverse economic circumstances, family disruption and behaviour problems are common among a great many deprived and delinquent adolescents, for entrants to the long-stay units this had been exacerbated by the failure of previous interventions.

Care and placement histories

The consequence of the difficulty in several areas of the young person's life was usually extensive involvement with specialist services, often necessitating long separation from home marked by frequent crises and placement breakdowns. As with so many aspects of this study, there were numerous interesting sub-groups.

For example, for three-fifths (58%) of those in state care, the current separation from home was their first. More startling still, 12% had been away from relatives for less than a year. This pattern was the one expected for the Section 53 grave offenders but when they were scrutinised, it was found that three-fifths (58%) of them had been in state care and all had spent extensive periods, usually on remand, in local authority secure accommodation or youth custody prior to getting into specialised treatment settings.

Whether they had been away for short or long periods, were in state care or sentenced under Section 53, all the young people had experienced some form of disruption and placement breakdown; as has been seen, for some it was a failure to be able to live at home; for others it was being expelled from a special boarding school (a quarter had been so placed); for some it was a failing at day school (62% those in state care and 14% of the Section 53 cases had been suspended); then there was the breakdown in foster care, children's homes, special adolescent units, other psychiatric settings, local authority secure units and even youth custody.

These findings on care and placement histories illustrate again the dangers of generalising about disturbed and problematic adolescents in specialist residential care establishments. What is true for most tends to be contradicted by a minority of other cases and any conclusions have to be hedged by qualification and disclaimer.

Establishing career routes

All that is presented in this chapter so far is essentially descriptive. The depressing lists of incidence rates of family difficulty, health problems, schooling deficiencies and anti-social behaviour are set out for the record. They are organised into the categories of life experience used in successive Dartington studies. They are summarised to give the essential picture (those wishing to look at the findings in full can find them in the *Journal of Forensic Psychiatry*, 1990). But they do not explain.

To make any progress, it was necessary to understand how these variables interact. Do young people whose parents have been over protective also have difficulties in other social relationships? And do they go on to commit serious offences? These life route interactions are fundamental to our understanding. Then it might be asked, do those who remain long in state care experience different patterns of living situations from those of the grave offenders and does this have a knock on effect for their education or their contact with health professionals? These are process interactions, to use the nomenclature of Chapter One. Then there is the way in which life route influences process; and vice versa.

The next step is to establish the dominant career route groups. By this is meant categories comprising young people who have had similar life experiences and involvement with specialist support agencies and who, therefore, might be expected to behave and respond to interventions in similar ways. The groups being sought are defined by their career routes rather than by their legal case status or by any psychological or psychiatric label they may have been given. The method for arriving at these categories incorporated analysing quantitative and qualitative information on the young person, taking a longitudinal perspective, and trying to capture the way in which risk and ameliorating factors across the young person's life interact. Five career groups emerged from this analysis.

Five career routes

The first comprised those who had been looked after away from home in state care for extensive periods since an early age. All had serious family problems and had exhausted the patience of a variety of foster homes and residential placements. Their increasingly disturbed behaviour had led to placement breakdowns and instabilities in school, causing social workers to seek, usually with reluctance, more controlling care environments increasingly distant from the young person's home area. There were 47 of these long-term child care cases.

The second group comprised 44 who had been long known to child guidance and special education and whose difficult behaviour and family situation had been of concern to teachers and psychologists. Usually, these children had been to a variety of special day and residential schools. Commonly, they were referred to social services by education departments at the age of 13 or 14 as a consequence of rapidly deteriorating behaviour and the need for a more controlling environment. These young people will be referred to as long-term special education cases.

Group three was made up of adolescents whose behaviour had come to the attention of welfare agencies fairly late, in their early or mid-teens, and whose behaviour had deteriorated so rapidly and to such an extent, that they moved quickly through a series of increasingly controlling regimes, usually ending up in local authority secure accommodation. While it is not unusual for children in mid-adolescence to surface with behaviour and delinquency problems, indeed Rutter's work would suggest that they have been hidden problem children for some time, the sudden appearance of these teenagers and their failure to respond to and their rapid exhaustion of all other interventions were alarming. While the eruption to the notice of statutory authorities was sudden, the underlying disruption was usually long-term, reflecting the increasing age and size of the young person, their failure in secondary school and the diminishing potential for family control. Adolescent erupters is the name given to the 30 adolescents in this group.

The 49 who comprised the fourth group were also hardly known to any agency. These one-off serious offenders had no previous involvement with welfare services and had never lived away from home prior to their committing a grave offence of homicide, arson or rape.

The final category included 34 persistent adolescent offenders who had regularly offended in their early and mid-teens and had eventually committed a grave crime which led to the placement in a secure treatment setting. Serious and persistent is a suitable label for these young people.

Having separated the 204 young people into these five groups, it was next necessary to ensure that the categories reflected differences in stress and ameliorating factors described earlier in the chapter. The testing involved two statistical techniques, the first being cluster analysis, which provides an understanding of the extent to which cases share similar characteristics, the second being discriminant analysis which determines the extent to which one group is different from another. Endless testing produced four variables which, in combination, best distinguished between the different groups of young people in the specialist treatment centres. These were:

- Number of times convicted in court

- Length of time in state care
- Length of time in residential schools
- Whether or not the young person had ever been to child guidance or child psychology services.

A dendogram of data clustered by Ward's (1963) method initially suggested that seven distinct groups of young people roughly analogous to the five just described are sheltered in specialist treatment centres. The following diagram summarises the patterns existing in each cluster.

Figure 4.1: The characteristics of seven clusters emerging from statistical analysis

	Seven Clusters						
Characteristics of Group	1	2	3	4	5	6	7
No. of convictions	Low	High	Low	Low	Low	High	Low
Time in state care	High	Low	Low	Low	High	Low	Low
Time in residential schools	Low	Low	Low	Low	Low	Low	High
Known to child guidance	Yes	No	Yes	No	No	Yes	Yes

The discriminant analysis subsequently showed that these seven categories could be legitimately amalgamated into the five career groups described above.

Clusters one and five   -   were predominantly long-term state care cases

Cluster seven   -   contained all the long-term special education cases

Clusters three and four -   were a mixture of the adolescent erupters who had only recently become involved with welfare agencies and those who had committed a single grave offence

Cluster two and six   -   contained all the persistent and serious offenders.

On balance, it seemed sensible to stick with the original five career groups. They have the quality of being distinctive, they amalgamate the process and life route dimensions described earlier and provide a sound basis for the predictive elements of the study to come.

The following table summarises the numbers of young men and women on each of the five career routes.

Table 4.4: Numbers of young men and women in specialised treatment centres by career group

	Long-term state care	Long-term special education	Adolescent erupters	One-off serious offenders	Serious & persistent offenders	Total
Young Men	29	37	15	44	30	155
Young Women	18	7	15	5	4	49
TOTAL	47	44	30	49	34	204

In subsequent chapters, the progress of these five groups will be compared. Knowledge about the likely development of different career routes from a group of young people studied retrospectively will be used to predict outcomes and to control for the relative contribution of background experience, individual circumstance and intervention to the progress of those in the prospective study. But, before getting this task underway, it is first necessary to describe the treatment experience. What happens to these young people when they get to a long-stay secure setting and what is their situation on the day of departure?

Conclusion

The young people in secure treatment centres are clearly a very heterogeneous group. Although they meet the criteria for placement in terms of disorder and danger, in all other aspects they are very varied. In education, for example, some are academically able and have done well at school, others can barely tell the time or handle money. Similarly, some have been long abandoned by their families while others continue to be supported by caring, concerned parents.

As a group, they display a higher than expected rate for almost every disadvantage and behavioural difficulty. However, no single characteristic dominates the population. It is difficult, therefore, to answer the question 'what sort of children enter secure treatment centres?' without going into their different backgrounds and developmental histories. A career perspective offers scope for understanding this array of data as in terms of life route and process the young people show some similarities and patterns can be discerned. Five career routes emerged from such an analysis and were confirmed when background factors were clustered statistically. These routes - long-term state care, long-term special education, adolescent erupters, one-off grave offenders and serious and persistent offenders - offer the best taxonomy for understanding what happens to the young people and will be used to analyse the follow-up data.

Having established the career routes and before asking what general outcomes can be expected for each one, it is necessary to describe the treatment approaches the young people are likely to experience.

5 The treatment experience

It has been established that there are some 130 extremely difficult and disturbed young people - as defined in this book - in England and Wales at any one time. Given our present scale of knowledge and technology, it seems that all of these youngsters have to be locked up. For most, stays in security for more than a year can be expected, occasionally for as much as five or even ten years. The specialised treatment centre can only be part of the recovery process; typically they will have the young person for about two years. The aim must be more than simple containment. Some difficult young people are placed in prison custody, but even here they experience something more than the standard fare offered to young offenders. But for those placed in a specialist treatment centre or long term secure unit more again in terms of therapy will be expected.

This chapter takes forward the analysis by attempting to answer four questions. First, what can be done for adolescents in these situations? That is to say what technology is available and what is the limit of current understanding. Second, what is done to help or, put another way, what is the practical interpretation of psychological and psychiatric theories? For this, evidence from one of the intensive studies of 56 young people prospectively followed through specialist treatment centres is used. Third, what change occurs during a typical stay in specialist treatment centres? As we shall see in Chapter Ten, the amount of change attributable to the residential intervention is calculated. Fourth, what is the situation of the 204 young people just described at the end of their treatment programme?

What can be done?

There is considerable misunderstanding about what can and is being done at specialist treatment centres. The psycho-therapeutic and psychological nomenclature does not always help nor is it easy for outsiders to grasp how theoretical principles are applied in a secure residential context. Moreover, as the coming pages demonstrate, there are unintended consequences of treatment seldom charted in text books. The starting point must be a brief overview of the theories which guide places like Aycliffe, Gardener Unit, Glenthorne, Vinney Green and Redbank.

Broadly speaking, as has been seen, problem behaviour displayed by the subjects of this book is generally regarded as indicating a psychiatric disorder (conduct disorder, emotional or mixed emotional and conduct disorder) of mainly psychological origin. For the sake of clarity, the two principal explanations of such disorder will be juxtaposed; first that which rests on *environmental* factors, looking for example at the way certain learned behaviours can be modified. Second, *psycho-analytic* theories which emphasise the importance of repressed or unconscious motives which have, if possible, to be brought to consciousness before a recovery can be achieved. These two theories are not by any means mutually exclusive; nor are they exhaustive.

Environmental explanations

Widespread experiments with animals have led psychologists to believe that behaviour is responsive to the environment and that human action can be learned and 'unlearned'. Pavlov introduced the ideas of operant conditioning and modelling, that the incidence of a particular behaviour will increase if it is followed by a reward or reinforcement and will decrease if followed by some form of punishment. Difficult behaviour is explained either as the failure to learn ordinary social skills or by the learning of specific deviant skills, for example, petty delinquency, often in a reinforcing cycle. Some have proposed the idea of streetwise skills which are appropriate to a particular environment but are maladaptive elsewhere.

Simply stated, those applying this environmental model in the treatment of children seek to reinforce appropriate behaviour with pleasurable consequences and to reduce inappropriate behaviour by withdrawing treats. In practice, such treatments tend to take three forms. Behaviour is modified by, for example, a system of punishment and rewards for specified actions. Then there are social learning programmes which seek to provide children with social skills to accomplish day to day behaviour and to reject opportunities to be anti-social. Finally, children have been encouraged, without any direct reinforcement, to model their behaviour on the orthodox and to reap the social rewards that generally accrue.

Clearly, there is a lot of common-sense in this environmental model; most people would own up to adapting their behaviour according to social rewards and punishments. The approach is wide ranging and has been applied in many contexts; indeed success has been claimed for several groups of problem children from arsonists to bed-wetters. Positive results can be achieved rapidly. On the other hand, 'behaviourists' as they have become known, have been criticised for a failure to maintain short-term achievements and for the lack of any clear association between treatment and effects.

Psycho-analytic explanations

The psycho-analytic approach to children's behaviour gives much greater salience to the underlying personality of the child as it develops in the first months and years of life. The personality structure of the child is thought to change little in its essentials during subsequent years. Stress is placed upon what Freud termed 'intra-psychic' phenomena, those aspects of the child's early rearing which become subsumed into its unconscious but continue to influence later interaction with the family and, as a consequence, the child's behaviour. Based on an analysis of adult memories of childhood, Freud focused upon the first six years of the child's life defining what he called the oral, anal and genital stages of development. These theories were developed in literature by Winnicott, Balbernie, Anna Freud, Klein and Dockar-Drysdale, all of whom worked directly with children.

Although diverse, psycho-analytic theory always stresses the importance of past relationships upon current patterns of interaction. Several psychological processes in child development, such as transference of emotions and regression to infancy as well as coping mechanisms also feature prominently in the literature. In each of these processes, the inter-generational aspects of psycho-analytic theory are clear so that practitioners frequently allude to the effects of grandparents upon mother-child relationships or even third generation interactions. The importance of sibling position is also evident since a parent's relationship with the first born invariably differs from the second, third, *et cetera*. The analytic theory of unconscious mechanisms motivating behaviour was refined in Dockar-Drysdale's writings and in the practical therapy of Balbernie by developing concepts such as the unintegrated or frozen child.

Behaviour modification

So much for the basic principles which underpin environmental and psycho-analytic explanations for children's problems. How have they been adapted and applied in specialist secure treatment contexts? Environmental approaches usually take the form of social learning models, particularly behaviour modification. Probably the most well known form of behaviour modification within residential centres is the 'token economy'. The basis of these schemes is that each child is held personally responsible for his or her own behaviour. Increasingly demanding targets are set for each individual which, if reached, are rewarded with tokens or points exchangeable for outings, goods, sweets, shampoo or other benefits, for example a more pleasant room. The essential aspects of residential life such as food or contact with relatives should be excluded from this regime. The use of behaviour modification with adolescents has been reviewed at centres such as Aycliffe, Glenthorne and Orchard Lodge.

Other techniques have been incorporated into the social learning repertoire. Contracts, sometimes written out and formally signed, between staff and child are tried. Programmes for developing social skills are extensively used. There are in addition packages designed to encourage the young person to re-examine offending behaviour, enhance job-hunting and independent living skills and to improve personal hygiene and self-appearance.

Behaviour modification, like any treatment programme can be misused and many have asked whether the use of rewards and punishments in residential settings is ethical. Critics have warned that what is considered a reward for good behaviour can actually be a young person's right. The denial of food, clothes or home visits would never be contingent on satisfactory behaviour but where do books, magazines, computers and other media fit into the picture? Applying the approach to children adept at manipulating adults also causes difficulty. Not infrequently, 'tokens' become part of an informal and largely deviant economy; and most difficult adolescents prefer cigarettes or other drugs to shampoo. Finally, modelling rests uneasily with the usual tensions about language, smoking, dress and sexual relations common in residential settings. Rewards for a cessation of violent behaviour might well be withdrawn as a consequence of an illicit kiss with another resident.

On the other hand, behaviour modification encourages staff to look at the individual needs of children and to explore the intricacies of the child's pathology. Such programmes have introduced the concept of reward into settings where hitherto punishment has been pervasive. It also gives a common focus for the different staff groups in the residential setting and impels them to evaluate their interaction with young people. Recipients tend to warm to behaviour modification programmes as progress is both understandable and measurable.

Behaviour modification techniques are used extensively in several secure treatment centres. Typically, the programme will begin with assessment. Short-term goals will be set, for example, to stop violent behaviour, but required skills improvement may be extensive, sometimes including learning to read. In a projected two year stay, the assessment might continue for as much as three months and will result in the young person being allocated to an appropriate treatment unit.

A visit to a centre professing to practice behaviour modification will usually reveal an environment in which personal, social work skills are frequently stressed. Every day, staff will assess the young person's behaviour in the context of agreed short and long-term goals. Performance will be graded and, at the end of every week, results combined and residents placed on one of several levels. Privileges are given to those at the top; benefits are withdrawn from those at the bottom. Excepting crises, young people usually only move up or down one grade every week. The desired direction of change is towards open facilities, mainstream education, work experience and, ideally, reunion with relatives or established independence.

Little of this will be helpful if it takes place in isolation from the outside world. An effective secure unit will also seek to ensure that the family remains involved in the young person's life. Naturally, any placement will meet its obligations set out in the *Children Act*, 1989 guidance to deal with family problems that arise. Liaison with the field social worker or probation officer is therefore important. However, behaviour modification approaches seldom attempt to link family problems with the young person's pathology, as would be common in psycho-therapeutic regimes. The aim is more to provide practical advice and support.

There will also be personal social skills training. Such work is varied in its methods and focus. It may address personal needs of the young person, such as hygiene; it can focus on emotional deficits, for example, to increase confidence; there are strategies to help relaxation and reduce anxiety and young people are taught how to manage their anger. Life skills, say how to shop or how to do laundry, and interaction skills, particularly between the sexes, also form part of the curriculum. Much of this work takes place in groups. Observed improvements are often tested out in educational visits to theatres, art galleries, museums and sporting events which are an integral part of the life of a good secure treatment centre.

Many behaviour modification treatment regimes are quite benign. They tend to be pragmatic in their application. Although behaviour modification and psycho-therapeutic regimes differ in their ethos and underlying principles, when applied in a residential context, methods tend to contrast by degree rather than by type. This proposition can be explored further with a discussion on the application of psycho-therapeutic approaches.

Psycho-therapeutic approaches

Whilst behaviour modification focuses upon specific aspects of the child's behaviour and specifies goals, psycho-therapeutic regimes focus upon the 'whole child'. The treatment seeks to understand all the elements in a young person's life and to explore the relationships between them. Thus whilst a resident's principal presenting problem may be a single grave offence, the treatment looks beyond this to relationships at home, in school and in the neighbourhood. The residential community is also seen as one system, leading Balbernie to describe the 'healing boundaries' which were placed around the

Cotswold Community. This approach to troubled children flourished between the wars and again in the 1960s and some, for example the Caldecott Community, Peper Harow and the Mulberry Bush, developed international reputations. However, not all have survived.

Staff and residents are often accorded similar status in a psycho-therapeutic regime, for example, being known as 'members of a community'. A variety of forums is established to encourage interaction and a rich environment of confrontation is fostered. The residents are encouraged to interpret their own and others' behaviour. This self-monitoring also extends to staff and, indeed, workers often monitor the effects of individual children upon their own situation by seeking external counselling or psycho-analysis. Needless to say, the intellectual and emotional demands upon all those in such residential centres are considerable.

Contrasts with behaviour modification became apparent almost from the day of entry to secure accommodation. In psycho-therapeutic contexts, young people seldom enter an assessment unit nor is steady progress towards open conditions expected. Within established legal confines, residents are allowed varying degrees of mobility both within and outside the living units. The consistency expected in behaviour modification regimes is frequently absent in a psycho-therapeutic centre. The social environment of the placement will be structured by the staff and young people who are invited to join the 'group' as they feel capable. The approach is manifest in the language used to describe the various parts; 'group workers' attempt to provide a 'total living situation' which continuously attempts to 'achieve insights' into the young person's life and 'to effect positive change'. Frequently, progress in one area can herald a crisis in another and the young person's life can become a roller coaster of ups and downs which are variously interpreted as depressing by the funding authority (which struggles to monitor development) and optimistic by the treatment centre (which measures progress by the number of crises overcome).

Any psycho-therapeutic environment, whether or not it is secure, will function around numerous meetings and the collection of documentary evidence on each child and 'the group'. There are usually weekly staff support meetings and treatment meetings between staff and residents. There will be daily business meetings on each unit and thrice daily 'change-over' meetings at which the group's progress is reported. In addition, there will be less frequent gatherings between those in residence and representatives from outside, for example, at three-monthly reviews or in family diagnostic sessions in which key family members attempt to gain some insights into their behaviour and, in turn, help to make the child's difficulties comprehensible. This technique is extensively used in family therapy. Documentary evidence extending from a daily log of significant events to carefully written statutory reviews is considerable.

What is done to help extremely difficult and disturbed young people?

These models for understanding and treating difficult and disturbed adolescents are based on contrasting, some would say conflicting, psychological theories. However, when adapted for use in institutions, the specific methods developed from environmental and psycho-analytic models have many similarities. Family work, clear and realistic expectations about acceptable behaviour and discipline, high standards and warm relationships between staff and residents should be a feature of good residential care whatever its professed treatment approach; these features may be as important to positive outcomes for the young people as the treatment ideology.

Data were collected on the treatment experience of all 204 young people in the principal follow-up studies. For the 102 in the retrospective study, information was inevitably limited. However, for the 56 young people prospectively followed from entry to Glenthorne and St Charles Youth Treatment Centres until they had left for at least two years, the treatment interventions were fully assessed. The following results are based on the experience of these youngsters.

Were the high ideals of treatment set out in preceding pages achieved? The analysis shows that any gains were hard won. Improvements in young people's functioning can be attributed to the work of the specialist centre. But it is folly to assume that behaviour modification or psycho-therapeutic work is in itself a solution.

It was encouraging to find that there were clear attempts to match interventions to the different needs of young people. The following table summarises the focus work in terms of the time and resources allocated to it for each of the five career groups. Naturally, the reduction of anti-social behaviour and the general calming of residents is important for all. But those long separated from home, either in the care of social services or special education, were offered increased levels of family work, while the concern with adolescent erupters and one-off serious offenders centred more on their psychological health.

Table 5.1: The primary focus of early work within specialised treatment centres by the career route of the young person

Focus of Work	% Long-term care	Career Group			
		% Long-term Spec. Ed.	% Adolescent erupter	% Serious one-off	% Serious & persistent
Living Situation	4	5	7	7	5
Family Relationship	19	16	23	16	21
Other Relationships	13	6	5	1	14
Anti-Social Behaviour	39	44	24	33	26
Physical Health	3	1	2	3	1
Psychological Health	7	14	24	22	11
Employment	7	1	4	6	4
Education	8	13	11	12	19
	100	100	100	100	100

Not only did the primary focus of the intervention reflect the needs of each resident, it also changed to meet their developing circumstances. Naturally, the principal concern with offenders is to calm their delinquent or violent potential. But once they are quiescent, the focus of attention must move on. Towards the end of their stay the work concentrates most on family relationships, where the young person will live and how they will adjust to the outside world. The range of work undertaken with residents, illustrated in the following table, was impressive. Hard bitten researchers used to the grandiose claims of residential centres which, on closer inspection, have little to offer other than simple bed and board, take some convincing but the specialist treatment centres clearly had something to offer.

Table 5.2: The proportion of residents benefiting from different types of interventions at some point during their stay in specialised treatment settings

Psycho-therapeutic (individual)	73%	Practical family work	80%
Psycho-therapeutic (family)	36%	Social skills training	89%
Medical intervention	13%	Offence counselling	70%
Education/Employment	70%	Drug/Alcohol counselling	25%
Security	16%	Stress-therapy	55%
Return Living situation	45%	Cultural stimulation/interests	85%

Continuity in treatment plans was also apparent. Only eight of the 56 residents were, at some point in their stay, without a coherent treatment plan. There were however, different patterns in the intervention of the two centres used for this part of the study. At Glenthorne, a clear path was marked through assessment, to treatment, to placement in the open unit and eventual release. At St Charles, assessment, treatment and future plans seemed to be a feature of each young person's day. Here, the intervention seemed to create crisis which then formed the subject of further treatment. This continuing fluctuation in young people's fortunes was recorded at length in young people's files.

A danger of any intervention is that it will become too inward looking and ignore the world outside to which residents will eventually return. Again, there were contrasts between the two centres in which the young people lived. Probation officers and social workers were frequently confused by the psycho-therapeutic terminology used to describe the St Charles regime. Indeed, the neutral observer was struck by the arrogance of many staff who gave the impression that they were the only people who 'knew' the residents' needs, prognoses and other circumstances. Administrators charged with justifying the expense of these interventions were judged harshly indeed: they were often credited with no understanding of the problems young people faced. Had these sentiments been clearly expressed or grounded in some evidence they might have been received more sympathetically. At Glenthorne, in contrast, outsiders were welcomed and easily understood the principles of treatment, and research evidence would be forwarded to visitors questioning the benefits of behaviour modification. At St. Charles, one was either a believer or an enemy. So one centre tended to look in and shun outside interest, while the other was more prepared to look out.

On the other hand, in both places, outside visits by residents for education, work, holidays and home visits were frequent, although naturally the mobility of grave offenders was restricted. However, there was only one case in which treatment plans were seriously affected by limitations on mobility imposed by the Home Office, a pattern that in some part reflects the caution of the Centres' treatment.

These data would suggest that, by different routes, both Centres are able to make some progress even with the most unpromising recruits. The impact of these efforts on long-term outcomes can be judged later. For now, it is enough to report that young people frequently forged close bonds with these establishments. A quarter maintained enduring relations with staff after leaving and 16% kept in close touch with other residents. But the stability achieved in the centres should not deflect attention from the size of the task that staff face nor the difficulties that must be overcome in order to secure gains. A fifth of the residents violently attacked staff during their stay and another 13% made a serious attack on the fabric of the building, including one boy who managed to inflict hundreds of thousands of pounds of damage to the unit in which he lived. Despite extremely close supervision, three of the 56 young people managed to attack a member of the public while on the books of these two centres.

Given the clientele, the risk of continued delinquency during residents' stays was inevitably high. Almost a fifth (16%) were convicted of a property offence and the same proportion of other offences while in the Centres. Nine young people had their sentence amended because of misbehaviour. It has been said before that, although they are secured, the young people are not always under lock and key. Over a quarter (29%) ran away during trips out of their placement but in only one of these cases did the young person commit an offence. Abuse of drink or drugs, on the other hand, was more common and affected 11% of residents.

What changed during the stay in treatment?

Stays in the specialised centres are long. The mean stay for the prospective entrants was just over 26 months and a fifth (18%) were resident for over three years. While it is to be hoped that the treatment plans just described will have an effect on the young person's future progress, there were other factors to take into account. Residents matured and became better equipped to cope with the demands of school and work. The very fact of being away from home or unsatisfactory substitute care arrangements had positive effects on the psychological health of some young people. The respite afforded to parents encourage them to review relationships with their offspring. Against this, new problems emerged, for example the discovery of past sexual abuse or the diagnosis of once latent mental illness.

Daily life in a secure unit also had its effect on residents' development. Young people formed relationships with one another and reflected upon their sexuality. The mix of residents at any one moment is vital to the atmosphere of the unit in which the young people live.

For example, extended discussion has focused on the ethics and efficacy of placing female victims of child sexual abuse in a situation where they are not only with but also outnumbered by male sex offenders.

Many commentators have noted that, despite considerable resources and good attention to detail, a secure treatment setting is not a natural place to spend adolescence. It frequently benefits the young person and is certainly better than prison, but it is far from normal. The absence of ordinary role models, the anxiety of living in a small space with extremely damaged people and the physical and emotional distance from home all militate against the best effects of treatment. This was illustrated by one young woman who had been sexually abused by her father suffering enormous guilt because he died in hospital before she was able to see him. All therapeutic efforts were undermined and the resentment that this young person harboured for those who 'kept her from her father' was clearly evident.

The legal status of many residents changed and this had its effect on the treatment intervention. It has been seen that those in state care have their secure accommodation order reviewed every six months, requiring professionals to put a strong case to the courts. Seven per cent of young people so detained were moved prematurely because the courts were not convinced that a further period in security was justified. In one case, this had disastrous consequences. In order to satisfy the court, but against the wishes of staff, a young person was moved to open conditions to prepare for release. Returning from a journey to work, he raped and seriously injured a woman, an offence punished by a sentence of life imprisonment.

Those subject to Section 53 sentences have their movements closely monitored by the Home Office. The decision to release a young person on licence or into prison facilities rests with the Home Secretary and advisors. Although treatment staff are asked for their opinion, they must accept the decision made in London and communicate it to the young person. In fact, as already described, in only one case did arrangements for mobility affect treatment plans but in 18% of Section 53 cases, there were differences of opinion over the manner and timing of the young person's departure and for all serving such a sentence tensions rose considerably as the end of their specialised treatment programme neared.

A premature departure occurred in one case in which a young person successfully appealed against his Section 53 sentence. Of low intelligence and from a large and extremely deprived family, this young man had been encouraged by a group of friends to set fire to what appeared to be a pile of old wood but turned out to be specialist railway sleepers valued at £200,000. Six months after entering secure accommodation, a three year sentence was turned into a two year supervision order, a decision which seemed legally and morally correct but which also deprived him of treatment that might have been beneficial.

Naturally, the psychiatric and psychological health of the young people was closely monitored. Over half of residents benefited from a concerted input from the consultant psychiatrists associated with the treatment centres. The psychological health of residents was more likely to improve (38%) or stay the same (24%) than it was to fluctuate (22%) or deteriorate (16%). Nonetheless, self-destructive behaviours were evident for nearly a quarter (22%) of the young people and six were hospitalised as a result of such activity at some point during their stay.

As has been found by much contemporary child care research, there was a depressing lack of attention to young people's education needs. While progress with deep-seated social and psychological problems is to be welcomed, it is disquieting that, despite being resident for two years or more, less than a fifth pursued education courses to the end and only 15% managed to secure qualifications such as City and Guilds (11%), BEC (5%), GCSE or A Levels (7%). Disappointment with this aspect of the Centres' work was partially offset by the considerable efforts made to find work experience situations and it is encouraging to find that nearly two-fifths (38%) had a full or part-time job outside of the treatment centre in which they lived.

Bringing this data together, it was possible to make an assessment of the effects of the treatment process upon young people's long-term prospects. It was found that only four departed without having an opportunity to benefit from the support on offer. In no case did the specialist treatment centre reduce life chances. Given the sophistication, quality and sheer expense of the intervention, this finding may appear trite or at least unsurprising. But it is more than is found in many other contexts and it is more than has been achieved for many of these young people in the past.

In over three-fifths of cases, the placement helped the young person's prospects in some way and for a third the intervention markedly improved the chances of satisfactory re-integration into society. Specialist treatment can make headway with even the most damaged child, even with the one of the four who departs prematurely. Against this, there remains a group of 21 young people who emerged little changed by treatment experience; as later chapters show, these youngsters depart at a considerable disadvantage to their peers.

Table 5.3: The benefit received from the specialised treatment intervention for young people leaving prematurely and staying full term

Stay	CONTRIBUTION			
	Changed and helped	Helped but did not change	Neither helped nor changed	Total
Full-term	19	15	18	52
Terminated prematurely	0	1	3	4
TOTAL	19	16	21	56

Young people's situations at the end of their stay

All but two of the 13 young people sentenced to indefinite detention were transferred to prison or youth custody centres, but 95% of those on determinate sentences were paroled. Most of those in state care returned to live in the community, either with relatives or in accommodation found by social services. Only four young people were completely free agents, in the legal sense, at the time of leaving. However, the time available for statutory oversight was usually short. With an average leaving age of 17.4 years, social services inputs could only be short-term (usually expiring at 18 years with some oversight possible to 21). For those paroled, the time gaps were larger and some sentences had as much as two-fifths to run.

On leaving, a third (30%) of residents returned to live with relatives or their immediate families, 10%, mostly boys, to foster homes and 12% to lodgings or their own accommodation, half of whom lived alone. The remaining cases left direct for another residential establishment; (16% to hostels, 4% to community homes, 22% to prison or youth custody, two to a Special Hospital and one to a mental hospital). These findings illustrated the interdependence between specialist treatment centres and other social services, health and penal provision.

Conclusion

Much has been said but little has been written about specialist treatments for extremely difficult and disturbed young people. Psycho-therapeutic settings have been especially reticent to commit ideas to paper. The gap between theory and practice for most interventions is considerable. Although it was not part of the analysis, visiting the various placements available for British youngsters and a handful of settings abroad, we got the impression that the facilities at Youth Treatment Centres were better than most. Nonetheless, many professionals felt they still fell short of text-book practice.

Thirty years ago, a study of this type would draw to a close here or possibly venture a little further into the offending behaviour of leavers. Today that is not sufficient. The next stage is to describe what happens to the young people in these placements, focusing on all areas of their lives. Then it is necessary to explain the outcomes and to understand why some leavers do better than others. For this, we return to the career groups identified in Chapter Four and establish from the retrospective follow-up data the general outcomes for each. In the next chapter the focus is on living situations, family relationships, education and employment and in the subsequent one on social and anti-social behaviour.

6 The two years after specialised treatment interventions

What were the outcomes for young people of a sojourn in a specialist treatment centre? This research has included long-term follow ups of a variety of groups of young people. The progress of some is still being charted, now nearly ten years since they came into the Centres: but these outcomes need not trouble us here. Let us explore what happened to the 204 young people; to find out where they lived, how they got on with their birth family, whether they established their own family and whether they got a job or any qualifications.

Some of those commissioning or helping to get the research underway did so with some trepidation. What would be found? On the negative side, four young people died during follow-up (although not all within two years of departure). This included one of the handful of young female AIDS victims in the UK. There was another young man who was stabbed through the heart with a pair of gardening shears by a fellow prisoner. A morbidity rate of one in fifty is higher than the national average although lower than had been feared by those working with these youngsters. Another two have been convicted of murder and are now locked up for life and eight have found their way into long-stay mental health facilities. Five more committed serious sexual offences.

Then there are the remarkable changes for the better. There was the boy who was out of control at 16 who settled down to successfully look after a schizophrenic wife and their baby son. There are young murderers who returned to their home community and were never again convicted. There were those who attacked and seriously inured their parents prior to placement and were later reconciled with them. For every sensational disaster there is at least one sensational success. But most hover in-between.

Where do leavers live?

This question can be answered in several ways. The easiest is to take a snapshot, at six months, a year or two years. Like happy family photos this can be deceptive but it is a start. The picture at two years reflects the increasing age and maturity of the young person. Only one in twelve are in the local authority settings, residential and foster care, that have been so much a part of their recent lives. Just under a quarter are in prison, a proportion swelled by the 34 leavers - nearly all one-off serious offenders - who moved straight from special treatment centre to prison or youth custody and remained there.

The greatest proportion (27%) are at home two years on; and another 3% live with other relatives, aunts, uncles, brothers, sisters and grandparents. This is the most likely destination for the adolescent erupters and serious one-off offenders who, of the five career route groups, have spent the least time away from home. A similar sized group (30%) have found some form of independence, mostly in their own flat, indicating a minimum of external support.

Table 6.1: Living situations of leavers two years after departure

	%
Prison custody	23
Secure hospital	6
Residential Child Care	1
Other hostels	5
Independent accommodation	30
Parents home	27
Foster parents	2
Other	5
Homeless	0
Dead	0
	N=204

Put a series of snapshots together and we get a movie, a very different way of looking at people's lives. For graduates of specialised treatment centres it is a busy picture. Three-fifths (62%) moved regularly and a core of 16%, mostly long-term special education and long-term state care cases, moved on average once every eight weeks. The movement was usually from a family member - three-fifths of all leavers lived with relatives at some point during the first two years - to an independent context and sometimes mirrored the test and see attitude of ordinary young adults. For others, particularly boys who had been long-term in state care and the persistent and serious offenders, the pattern was of disruption and often involved spells in prison custody.

Even the 34 young people who remained in some form of custodial situation during the two years after leaving a treatment centre failed to find much stability. Ten did settle in a single young offender institution, usually one which had been selected to meet particular needs, for example social skills or employment training. But the others were shunted around the country so beginning a pattern that was to continue for as long as they remained locked up. Most of these were one-off serious offenders. Take these young people out of the equation and it is possible to state that movement in the years that follow a spell in specialist treatments centres correlates highly with movement prior to their entry. So, it is the long-term care cases and rejects of special education who find it hardest to settle, while the adolescent erupters who lived at home up until their 15th or 16th birthday move little during follow up.

It would be a mistake to reflect on these data and conclude that young people either settle at home or live independently; a stark contrast offered to many for whom the State has responsibility. It would certainly be wrong to think that those who live at home are happy while those that live away are not. These two types of living situations are frequently closely linked. It will be seen below that a significant proportion of young people continue to have troubled family and social relationships. But such youngsters are seldom happier away from home than they are within it. What is more, those that manage to get on with relatives and maintain some reasonable contact with them are usually the most successful at establishing an independent way of life. These findings concur with those found by Stein and colleagues in a different context.

These young people enjoy maximum support while in the Centres but it evaporates swiftly in the outside world. Less than a fifth of graduates were helped into a place to live by their social worker or probation officer. Most relied on relatives. Those that did get help usually got it from a member of staff at the specialist treatment centre whose involvement frequently extended well into the young person's adulthood. While such support is to be applauded it does not say much for the inter agency co-operation that one might expect for such difficult youngsters.

Family and social relationships

It was seen in the previous chapter that the treatment programme gives much attention to the young person's family. The result of this effort is encouraging, as many as a half of those scrutinised appear to have better insight into their family and social relationships at the end of their stay. But family members do not always make the same progress. A sizeable proportion, probably at least a quarter, carried on their lives much as they had in the past and learned little of their responsibilities.

As a consequence, careful monitoring of the family during the two years after the young person has departed specialist treatment interventions shows that two-thirds (65%) continue to have problems. This proportion includes the third who felt unable to go home or would be refused a bed by relatives if they asked. These findings are not as disquieting as they may at first appear. After all, stresses and strains are a feature of most families and the efforts of older adolescents to find an independent niche can hardly be counted as a protective factor. That said, what is found here is that young people leaving specialist treatment centres go back to families which have very similar characteristics to those which they left. The most that can be hoped for is that the young person has some insight into these difficulties and is therefore better equipped to cope.

It is unsurprising, therefore, to discover that patterns of contact between young people and their families fluctuate. Sometimes they are very close to each other. We have just seen that three-fifths of the 204 being described here actually lived with their relatives during their first two years after treatment. But even amongst this group there was a sizeable minority who spent extensive periods not only out of contact but also refusing to talk to any of their relatives. And one in seven of leavers did not see their parents at all during this period.

The highest levels of contact were found among the serious and persistent offenders. This finding is not unexpected. Repeated studies of family links shows that young offenders stay closer to their relatives even when relationships are less than ideal. Those young people who had been long in state care also maintained reasonable levels of contact compared to the remaining three career groups, but here the connection was more likely to reflect an absence of any better alternative than any intrinsic warmth between parent and child.

The lowest levels of contact were found for the one-off serious offenders who remained in prison custody throughout the follow up period. It will be remembered that most in this career group who were released went home to relatives. Many of those left in prison had committed grave crimes against family members. They had often failed to gain sufficient insight or express any remorse for their offence; and a parent might be excused for failing to visit a son who has tried to burn the house down with him or her in it. But even where progress was made, the potential for enriching family links was hindered by geographical impediment; we have already commented on the frequent movement of long-term prisoners around different establishments in the country.

Frequency of contact between young people and family members is a crude but effective measure of family relationships. But staying in touch is not the same as being close. Given the nature of the data collected on the young people being discussed here, it is not possible to talk about the depth and significance of family relationships with any confidence. Nonetheless, some indication was possible using measures used in other Dartington studies.

These tended to show that relationships within the young person's family were better than the patterns of contact and living situations indicated. The most handicapped group has been mentioned; those convicted of and failing to show any remorse for an offence committed against a family member. Then there are young people long in state care, particularly the boys in this group. They generally face the same problems at home as existed when they first left many years ago; and they behave in a way that exacerbates those problems.

But for other young people the climate at home generally improves. The long-term special education cases mature out of the problems that brought family members to their knees in earlier years and family relationships consequently improve. With the other career groups, family members frequently grow out of the problems they have posed for their off-spring; they become too exhausted to continue family discord, they retire from chronic unemployment or offending and they form new relationships with people who bring much needed diversions from the past.

Parents form new relationships and so do the young people. Five percent of graduates married within the two year follow-up and 10% became a parent themselves. This, of course, often changes the family dynamic. What a difference the transition to father or daughter-in-law can make to the power balance in a family; even a disordered family. What a difference the status of grandparent can make when family members consider the pros and cons of staying in touch.

This said, on the whole, extremely difficult and disturbed young people are not very good at making friends or forming enduring relationships. The one-off serious offenders who remain in prison have little opportunity and those who are released are understandably hesitant. The long-term state care and special education cases are gregarious but their relationships are seldom close; even when they cohabit. The persistent and serious offenders are seldom stable enough to make a lasting friend. Only the adolescent erupters seem capable of settling down and become happy in doing so.

Physical and psychological health

A higher proportion of graduates from specialist treatment centres suffer physical health problems than surveys of the general population would lead us to expect. Four of the 204 died after the two year follow up; this has been mentioned already. Two others suffered chronic physical illness. The first, a one-off grave offender developed an eye condition that threatened blindness. The second, a long-term care case had increasing problems of mobility; her poor psychological state aggravated her physical condition, in as much as she persistently injured herself, thus reducing treatment options. Eighteen suffered less serious conditions, including appendicitis, stomach ulcers, pregnancy complications, overdoses and injuries received in accidents or violent attacks. Seventeen more received treatments at clinics for problems as varied as deafness, venereal disease, psoriasis, epilepsy and asthma. All this within two years of leaving. The low numbers make calculations difficult but young people on the three career routes involving extensive involvement with state services had a higher morbidity than those who came to notice in adolescence.

One in ten of the leavers became parents within two years of leaving specialist treatment centres. For the young women becoming mothers this meant hospital admission. Fourteen of the 49 women had children, a much higher rate than found in the general population. For the long-term state care and special education cases the ratio was higher still.

There were no unusual complications in the 14 births and none of the babies had any obvious disability.

Some young people had physical health problems consequent upon their lifestyle or psychological health. One serious and persistent offender crashed the car he had stolen and was hospitalised. Seven more - six of these women who had been long in state care - were hospitalised after suicide attempts or overdoses. The same number - this time mostly young men - developed addictions to alcohol or drugs. Five of those experiencing periods of homelessness complained of deteriorating physical health.

The mental health of leavers was also worse than that of young people generally. Ten per cent developed conditions requiring extensive treatment; one per cent would have been a reasonable estimate had the general population been a guide. Latent mental illness that had probably contributed to the young person's problems in adolescence became manifest in the two years after leaving. One-off serious offenders had the highest mental health morbidity. In all, 18 of the 204 young people were admitted to mental hospitals, of whom twelve went to a secure establishment. Seven more developed an identifiable mental illness, such as schizophrenia, that required hospitalisation. Six of the grave offenders who moved directly from the treatment centres to youth custody were treated there by a psychiatrist.

In addition, there was the usual run of depression and anxiety that is associated with a disturbed childhood. In a few cases these patterns of bizarre behaviour were left largely untreated. One young woman who had been long in state care lived a life akin to that of an urban guerrilla, albeit one deprived of a gun. Another young man, who had once been in special education settings, now spent at least four hours a day sitting on a bus as it circumnavigated his home city. All of the grave offenders transferred directly to custody suffered depression and anxiety which was seen as a natural reaction to their living situation and so remained largely untreated.

Putting this evidence together, it can be said that a significant proportion of extremely difficult and disturbed young people suffer poor health well into adulthood. But the majority suffer no problems at all. And the nature of the health difficulty does appear to be differentiated between the five career routes, a finding that helps to predict outcomes in later chapters.

Education and employment

It was seen in the last chapter that the treatment centres' contribution to the education of difficult and disturbed young people was disappointing. This is reflected in progress on leaving. Just under one third (30%) took part in any education and most who started rapidly dropped out. It was the adolescent erupters who benefited most, followed by those serious one-off offenders who transferred directly from treatment centre to prison custody as part of a plan which eventually led to a return to the community. Young people sentenced to Section 53 sentences frequently get preferential access to classes in prison, a reflection of their length of stay compared to other young offenders.

This lack of educational development was mirrored in - and was sometimes the cause of - unemployment. We live in an era in which high proportions of disadvantaged youngsters fail to find work. Even so, it was dispiriting to discover that two-fifths of leavers and 54% of long term care cases never worked during the two year follow-up. Worse still, half of those who did secure a job left it within three days of starting; and those who were eased out of their jobs by employers were far outnumbered by those who drifted away voluntarily, unable to find the social skills necessary to put up with a hum-drum working life. Only eight young people secured skilled work of any kind in the two years after leaving the treatment centres; five of these were adolescent erupters.

Whatever progress is made with the family and social relations of extremely difficult and disturbed young people, or in the reduction of offending - the subject of the following chapter - lack of education and employment remains a considerable handicap in adulthood. With time, this is a deficiency that may come to undermine other aspects of the young person's life.

Conclusions

This description of the family and social relations, education and employment, physical and psychological health and living situations of 204 graduates from specialist treatment centres offers much room for encouragement. Certainly, progress is better than that predicted by experts when the study began. The question is 'what contribution do the specialist centres make to any progress made by the young people?' This chapter helps with an answer in as much as it provides a benchmark against which the progress of young people on the five career routes could be prospectively measured. The data described here was used to set out what could be achieved at best and worst for 56 young people for whom outcomes were unknown when the follow-ups began. This comes later. First, it is necessary to build in findings on the offending patterns of treatment centre graduates.

7 Social and anti-social behaviour in the two years after treatment

Much of society's concern with extremely difficult and disturbed young people centres on offending, particularly the repetition of serious and violent crime. Conviction during the two years after leaving treatment institutions is the benchmark most used to measure the efficacy of reformatory interventions. It is certainly true to say that gaining any personal insight into crime will count for little if offences continue.

In fact, reconviction rates from specialist treatment centres can be misleading. For a start, 10% of entrants had never been convicted. Eleven of the 204 followed here were convicted for the first time *after* leaving. Reconviction rates for prison department young offender institutions are generally in the range of 65% - 90%. But such places take young people with a criminal history, usually one which is long and illustrious; so it is to be expected that offending outcomes here will be worse than in specialist centres. In addition, 34 of the leavers described had little opportunity to offend because they were locked up for the entire two year follow-up. Thus, comparisons between different interventions are difficult to make.

The discussion of the social and anti-social behaviour of the 204 graduates of specialised treatment begins with simple misbehaviour and then explores who offends and the seriousness of the crimes committed. Subsequent calculations are made to find out how many of those who were at liberty during the two year period got into trouble; a figure which is a more realistic indicator of the treatment centres' ability to influence offending behaviour.

Behaviours not recorded by the police

Much of the difficult adolescent behaviour that necessitated admission diminished during the stay in treatment centres and did not recur. This improvement may be due to the intervention; a possibility that will shortly be explored. But the increasing age and changed circumstances of the young people also contributed to their improvement. For example, the poor educational progress just mentioned was not accompanied by truancy, as the leavers were well beyond school leaving age. Running away also ceased to be a problem and sexual acting out diminished as a concern, at least for those professionals with statutory responsibility for the child's welfare.

While some problems diminished, others persisted and new ones emerged. Four types of behaviour are sufficient to illustrate the predominant patterns. First there is use of drugs, including glue and gas. Second there is behaviour known to the police but not leading to a criminal conviction. Third is offending which evades police detection. And, finally, there is self-destructive behaviour.

Naturally, with such a vulnerable group of young people, substance abuse was a constant hazard. A quarter of leavers were known to use drugs, gas or glue, a proportion which increases to two-fifths (41%) for young men who had been long in state care. Commonly, the drugs and stimulants were cannabis, glue, gas and LSD but four young people became regular users of heroin. Several also had a problem with alcohol. Again, the incidence of problems is greater than in the wider adolescent population; yet the majority of leavers were not users of drugs.

A fifth (19%) of leavers displayed anti-social behaviour which was known to the police but did not lead to a prosecution. This situation was particularly common among girls from long-term state care and special education career routes. In many instances, the incident was considered too minor to warrant anything more than an informal caution or stern telling-off. But half of these young people were simply viewed as something other than offenders, either because their behaviour was bizarre or peculiar to family context. For example, one adolescent erupter deliberately damaged his parents' car after a row with his father. The police were aware of the financial costs already incurred by his parents and administered a formal caution at the scene. A girl, once placed for a long time in a special boarding school, developed an obsession in adulthood with the royal household at Sandringham.

Despite breaches of security that required the involvement of anti-terrorist police, no action was taken against the woman who was considered to be borderline mentally ill and was certainly not a threat to anybody.

Most young people offended on leaving specialist treatment. Some managed to evade detection. The crimes were minor, usually shoplifting and very occasional drug use. A third of those unconvicted by the time they had been out of treatment for two years - 15% of the entire sample - offended in such ways. Some of this crime was known to other agencies; there were housing officers responsible for sheltered accommodation who turned a blind eye to marijuana use. There were some probation officers who had strong suspicions that a young person was shoplifting but were insufficiently confident to take the matter forward. Most (53%) of these undetected criminals had been serious and persistent offenders prior to entering treatment, now they dabbled in very minor property crime. As far as the researchers were aware, there were no serious offences going undetected that could be attributed to the 204 young people.

Finally, there were those young people already described who tried, often successfully, to hurt themselves. Much of this was attention seeking behaviour, usually taking overdoses. Some isolated young people, particularly those who had been long in state care, committed crimes to get themselves noticed.

Conviction rates

Half (50%) of the 204 young people studied here were convicted within the two year follow-up. If we add to this the eight young people who committed offences in that period but were sentenced more than two years after leaving, the rate rises to 54%. Add the 15% who committed crimes never detected by the police and the rate rises to 70%. Boys long in local authority care along with serious and persistent offenders were those most likely to offend. Both of these categories comprised young people convicted three or more times in adolescence, whom we know are at the highest risk of continued delinquency in adulthood.

Table 7.1: Rates of conviction within two years of leaving for each career group

Long-term state care	62%
Long-term special education	59%
Adolescent erupter	57%
Serious one-off offenders	18%
Serious and persistent offenders	62%
	N=204

The low rates of one-off serious offenders convicted is misleading. They are, as will be seen, the least likely to commit a crime, even when released to the community. However, 13 were not let out of secure conditions during the first two years, and their only opportunity to offend was in prison or hospital, so the conviction rate is much depressed.

Serious crimes

In view of their previous serious and persistent deviant behaviour, a single burglary committed by one of these very difficult young people after leaving could be viewed as a significant improvement. In Chapter Four, the offences committed by the young people were categorised on a scale of seriousness. In category one there were the 8% of adolescents who had taken somebody's life. In category two were another 20% convicted of a violent crime with a sexual motive, such as rape or indecent assault. Lower down in category six there were those found guilty of offences which involve loss and/or damage to property but no personal injury to the victim. This includes criminal damage and burglary which is the most that 20% of the 204 young people had ever done. In category nine were the 10% who had never offended.

As one would hope, it is found that less serious crime is committed after departure from specialised treatment centre than before entry. They had nearly 16 years during which to do something terrible before being locked up and, by the measure used here, only two years of opportunity afterwards. Nevertheless, moving straight from the treatment centre to prison or hospital does not totally deter a leaver from crime; as has been explained, one graduate murdered his cell mate. The following table explores the nature of the offences committed by those leaving the centres within two years of leaving.

Table 7.2: Seriousness of offences for which young people were convicted during the first two years after leaving (all 204 cases)

Offence category	Proportion so convicted
	%
1. Loss of life	0
2. Violent with sexual motive	2
3. Violent with no financial motive	5
4. Property offences which involve personal injury	7
5. No personal injury but serious risk	2
6. Property offences with no personal injury	23
7. Loss of property and no personal injury	7
8. Victimless, non-acquisitive offences	3
9. No offence	50
	N=204

* Most serious offence only is recorded in this table

When a period longer than two years is considered, the number of young people committing grave offences increases. The circumstances of the two young people who committed murder within the two year period but were convicted later on require brief explanation. The first, David, behaved unpredictably. A classic adolescent erupter, he regularly attended school, performed well there and posed no real difficulty until a few months before his 15th birthday when he was convicted of a minor offence which alerted social services. In their care, David rapidly deteriorated to the point where local authority secure accommodation and then specialist treatment became a necessity.

In the latter he did well. So well, in fact, that the court in his local authority questioned the wisdom of extending the secure accommodation order and, against the advice of his carers, he was moved to open conditions. Soon afterwards, returning from a journey to work, he broke into a house, raped the woman occupier and battered her around the head with a hammer. He calmly returned to the Treatment Centre and it was several weeks before he was arrested. He was eventually sentenced to life imprisonment. In custody, he murdered a fellow prisoner by cutting his throat, using a razor blade secreted in his cell for several weeks.

The second case of murder involves a young man with several convictions for violence who was released from specialised treatment having served the entire two and half years of his sentence. He settled near home and, although generating considerable unease in his family and probation officer, stayed out of trouble for over 18 months and occasionally found himself work. He secured a flat in a large housing estate near to his parent's home. Several months later, he lured the rent collector, a young woman, into the flat and brutally murdered her. He was convicted and sentenced to life imprisonment with a recommendation that he serve at least 20 years.

Twenty-one young people were found guilty of offences in the same category as those which contributed or even precipitated the need for the specialised treatment. Only five of these 21 were serious crimes. These 'mirror' offences are of special concern and, again, are worth lengthier description.

> The first case involves a Section 53(2) graduate who, six months after leaving, attacked and raped a six year old mentally retarded girl, a friend of the family. This offence was almost a replica of that which had earned the previous Section 53(2) sentence and placement in a specialist centre. A further three counts of indecency were taken into consideration by the judge who passed a seven year youth custody sentence upon the offender.

> A girl convicted of kidnapping a baby prior to entering treatment, committed exactly the same offence 11 months after departure and was given a two year probation order. Although it was a serious case which caused great distress to the mother, no one else came to serious emotional or physical harm as a result of the offence.

> A boy with a history of violent behaviour towards men and sexual assaults on women repeated the pattern on leaving. As the offending was linked to violent fantasies, it was feared he would commit a grave offence. So far he has been convicted of indecent assault resulting in a three year prison sentence.

> A boy with a history of arson prior to entering the treatment centre, set fire to the hostel in which he was living 12 months after leaving. He was sectioned and placed in a mental hospital.

> A boy serving a six year sentence under Section 53(2) for rape escaped from the treatment centre and committed the same offence. The victim was a social worker who had worked with the offender in the past. A life sentence was passed.

Naturally, all would hope that either the specialist treatment intervention or continued detention in prison or hospital would ensure that no leaver again committed a grave offence. Unfortunately, this is not the case. Since, nearly 70% of the young people have been convicted of serious crimes in the past, by their very nature, they are always likely to be dangerous. If we were to look for a sample of murderers, rapists and arsonists in society, these young people would come high on the list of candidates - whichever of the five career routes being travelled. But the proportion confirming their dangerous nature by a repeat outrage is low; less than 1% are convicted of murder and less than 2% are convicted of rape.

The levels of other serious crime is also much reduced. It is the serious and persistent offenders who are most likely to be convicted of crimes which involve physical contact - usually violence - with the victim. Of the other four career routes, the long-term care and special education groups are also prone, although the low numbers hamper comparisons, to repeat offences. These points will be pursued in later chapters.

Standard conviction rates and sentences to custody

The general conclusion of the findings just described is that conviction rates appear to be reasonably low. In studies of approved schools, secure accommodation and prison custody, reconviction rates of 65 - 90% are common. In specialised treatment units, there are more serious crimes in the profiles of individual young people - indeed, this is the first study with which we have been involved where a leaver has murdered - but not more serious crime overall (the proportion of YOI graduates convicted of crimes which involve physical contact with the victim would be about the same).

But these conclusions would be viewed as unreliable by those used to standard conviction rates. Criminologists tend to look at the proportion of young people who had been convicted within two years of leaving specialised treatment centres, they would restrict themselves to only those young people who had been at liberty during the follow-up, those having opportunity to offend (although it has been seen that some of the treatment graduates were criminal in prison). To make a comparison between those difficult young people described here and those in other studies, for example, leavers from young offender institutions, we must exclude the 34 who left treatment for custody throughout.

Even then contrasts are doubtful. Many of the young people dealt with here are serious offenders who, if released to the community, are much less likely to get into trouble than the persistent property delinquents characteristic of prison custody. The specialist treatment centres also shelter youngsters who have never been convicted; offending outcomes for this group were unknown prior to this study, but they were not expected to be low nor were they found to be high.

Observing these caveats, we find the conviction rate for leavers at liberty at some point during the two years after leaving to be 60%. However, another 5% were convicted at later stages for crimes committed during the first two years after release. As the following table illustrates, rates are highest among boys from the long-term state and serious and persistent offender career routes. Both categories contain a high proportion of young men who had been convicted three or more times by their 16th birthday - the commonly accepted definition of a persistent offender - and who have suffered a disproportionate amount of isolation. The significance of these risk factors will become clear in the following chapter.

Table 7.3: Conviction rates within two years of leaving specialised treatment settings for the five career groups and for young men and women in each category *

	Male	Female	All
Long-term care	85%	44%	69%
Long-term education	72%	43%	67%
Adolescent erupter	79%	43%	61%
Serious one-off offender**	31%	0%	29%
Serious and persistent offender	69%	75%	70%
TOTAL	65%	44%	60%

* only young people at liberty at some point during two year follow-up included (N=170)

** Low numbers in this category make comparisons doubtful

Another measure favoured by criminologists - largely because it acts as an indicator of the seriousness of an offence - is the proportion of young people convicted and sentenced to custody within a two year period after their release from custody. Those followed up from specialist treatment centres are handicapped by this comparison because a previous record of serious crime can harden the courts' attitude in any subsequent disposals. There were several instances of serious and persistent offenders settling down in the treatment centre, being released to the community, committing a relatively minor offence and being sentenced to custody by an unsympathetic court. As the next chapter shows, young people from minority ethnic groups were especially prone to such unsympathetic treatment. Nonetheless, the analysis reaps the following results.

Table 7.4: Rates of sentence to custody within two years of leaving specialised treatment settings for the five career groups*

	All
	%
Long-term state care	26%
Long-term special education	44%
Adolescent erupter	21%
Serious one-off offender**	6%
Serious and persistent offender	23%
TOTAL (N=170)	25%

* only young people at liberty at some point during two year follow-up included

** Low numbers in this category make comparisons doubtful

Conclusion

At the point of entry to specialised treatment centres, the young people discussed here are an unenviable group. Nine out of ten had been convicted of offences and 70% had been found guilty of serious crimes before entry. In Chapter Five it was seen that while the young people are in the centres, their misbehaviour is much reduced and offending also diminishes. On leaving, the opportunities for general delinquency, getting into trouble with the police and further convictions increase; and a rise in offending behaviour during the two year follow-up has been found.

Seventy per cent of leavers offend in some way. Half are convicted within the two year period. A quarter are convicted of an offence which the court considers serious enough to warrant prison custody. Seventeen per cent are convicted of an offence that involves some physical contact between victim and offender - the research definition of a serious offence. Two (1%) are convicted of violent robbery and another five (2%) of rape.

Should we despair or rejoice at these outcomes? With respect to the grave offences they may be perceived as disastrous, since the goal has to be zero convictions. But in other ways, the findings are encouraging. Offending is less than might have been anticipated and, particularly important, serious crimes are much reduced. Indeed, when we come to compare 'like with like' in Chapter Eleven, it will be seen that specialist treatment centres appear to do better with these extremely difficult cases than do other secure units, such as those run by local authorities or young offender institutions run by the Prison Department.

The results given here have been largely descriptive but are important because they indicate some pattern to the outcomes. The career routes are clearly important in determining where people will live, whether they will get a job and whether they will get into trouble. Other factors, particularly gender, ethnicity and resilience to adversity are beginning to emerge as important. The next step in the analysis is to try to explain these outcomes, to find out why some young people do better than others. This forms the subject of the penultimate part of this book.

8 Predicting from extensive data

At the outset we looked at the background circumstances of extremely difficult and disturbed young people. Subsequently the interventions fashioned on their behalf have been described and an attempt made to gauge the consequences. Then we have explored outcomes, looking at what happened in the two years after the treatment came to an end. The purpose of this penultimate part of the study is to see if the information about background and treatment can be used to explain outcomes; to be able to predict who offends, who goes home to relatives or who achieves a reasonable quality of life as young adults.

There are two ways of fashioning prognoses: the first and most usual method is statistical. It uses the extensive data on the 204 cases to select variables which, in combination, correlate with outcomes. The second, much less common, is qualitative. This relies upon the intensive data on the 56 young people whose outcomes were unknown when predictions were made by the researchers. We forecast what would happen and waited to see what came about. Each method has its strengths and weaknesses. As the research has progressed we have come to the conclusion that the intensive approach is the most accurate. But the two are linked; the statistical findings helped in the making of predictions on individual cases and it is by adding up individual prognoses that the wider picture is assembled. Whatever their relative merits, both are sufficiently interesting to warrant their reporting here.

Let us first look at the statistical findings. We scrutinised four outcome variables. Given the public concern aroused by criminality, the two variables of the number of convictions and serious offending are important. Since family members influence a young person's success, the variable 'who goes home' has been selected. Finally, a composite outcome indicator was constructed to give an overview of all aspects of the young person's situation two years after leaving the treatment centre; where he or she lived, how they got on with family and friends, what their health was like, where they were being educated and whether they were employed.

Who gets convicted?

It was seen in the previous chapter that 50% of all leavers and 60% of those who had an opportunity to offend in the community were convicted within two years of leaving treatment centres. In addition, another 4% committed offences in the study period but were convicted later on. Needless to say, innumerable factors are statistically associated with the outcome. Not all of these indicators are very useful. For instance the finding that healthy graduates are more likely to get into trouble than those suffering physical illness may be of academic interest but it is hardly the basis for a practice innovation. More helpful - but not particularly surprising - was the discovery that those most likely to offend were young people who had failed to benefit from the intervention, were male, had been long in state care, previously in trouble with the law and were perceived as socially isolated. More surprising was the finding that fewer of those experiencing psycho-therapeutic interventions were found guilty of an offence than those under behaviour modification regimes.

By themselves, these factors do not tell us very much. Many of the indicators may be related to one another. For example, if all those getting behaviour modification had been persistent male delinquents also previously in state care, the finding that two-thirds (67%) of such graduates were convicted in the follow-up period compared to just under half (48%) of those leaving psycho-therapeutic environments and at liberty to offend would not be of any significance. To take the analysis forward, factors associated with a criminal conviction were grouped into three; those to do with the young person's enduring characteristics, such as ethnic background and intelligence; those which described his or her background, for example the career route and the frequency of previous convictions and, finally, those factors to do with the treatment intervention.

In order to explore the factors that predict offending most accurately, the 34 young people who remained in custody throughout the follow-up period were excluded from the analysis and the eight who offended during the study period but were convicted later on were classified as offenders. Thus, the analysis was based on 170 young people of whom 110 were convicted of offences committed within two years of leaving the centres. Some factors that closely correlated with others in each group (and therefore had little explanatory power) were excluded. Those that were left were tested using logistic regression techniques best suited to the type of data (categorical) being analysed. The results were somewhat surprising. Six variables, in combination, best predict whether or not a young person will be convicted within two years of leaving a specialised treatment setting; these are, gender, whether the young person stayed full term, whether the young person lived at home during the study period, the quality of their social relationships as they left the treatment centres, the centre attended and their career route. The following table shows the results.

Table 8.1: Log-linear logistic regression analysis of variables associated with conviction within two years of leaving a secure treatment centre

Variable	Coefficient	Standard error	Significance	Odds
Gender	1.44	.49	.003	4.21
Stayed full-term	1.29	.68	.057	3.62
Lived at home	1.27	.50	.012	3.55
Integrated socially	1.02	.39	.009	2.76
Centre attended	0.67	.40	.089	1.96
Career route:				
Long-term care	1.23	.42	.004	3.41
				21.51
Long-term special educ.	-0.10	.36	.773	0.90
Erupters	0.18	.41	.656	1.20
One-off serious offender	-1.74	.40	.000	0.18
Serious and persistent offender	0.43	.42	.306	1.54

This evidence suggests that young men who left treatment prematurely, lived at home at some point, were poorly intergrated socially, experienced a behaviour modification regime and had long been in state care over 21 times more likely to be convicted than if opposite conditions apply. Particularly interesting in this context is the independent effect of the treatment regime. Residential regimes are generally not thought to be closely associated with re-offending after release (Cornish and Clarke, 1975) and cognitive approaches are usually associated with successful interventions with young offenders (Lipsey, 1992). Very difficult and disturbed young people at this stage of their career appear to be exceptions to this rule, a finding that echoes those of Marshall's results (1997) for leavers from Grendon Underwood therapeutic prison.

The weakness of statistical analysis is the crude way in which variables are constructed. Findings therefore require careful interpretation. The results on social relations are only possible by classifying individuals as being either 'well' or 'poorly' integrated (since any other division produces categories too small to compare). Looking at cases one by one suggests a plethora of reasons why poor social relationships might be a disadvantage and why the 'process' serves such young people so poorly. For example, they may be generally disliked and present themselves unfavourably to assessment agencies and courts. Describing an intervention as either 'behaviour modification' or 'psycho-therapeutic' is also an over-simplification for the reasons given in Chapter Five.

Nonetheless, there are likely explanations of outcome being uncovered here. These can be explored by a second statistical analysis (CHAID) which identifies sub-groups that are particularly prone to success or failure. When this is applied to the same 170 young people, it is found that nine-tenths (92%) of young men that have been long in care are convicted within two years of leaving compared with 32% of young women who were well adjusted socially. The following table depicts the situation, demonstrating just how complicated the patterns underlying the statistical divisions can be.

Table 8.2: The proportion of young people in different sub-groups convicted within two years of leaving specialised treatment centres

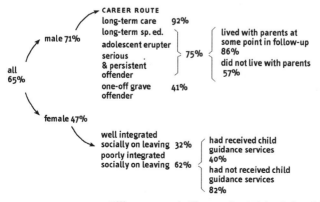

Differences are significant at the 95% level of confidence

It can be seen that gender is clearly related to reconviction but that this effect is more marked for some groups than others. Those young men who were persistently delinquent prior to entry are especially likely to offend but further differences emerge when living at home with parents is added to this variable. It is then found that leavers who are in the long-term special education, adolescent erupter and serious and persistent offender career groups and who live with parents at some point during the follow-up study display almost as high a reconviction rate as those on the long-term care career route, the most vulnerable group of all. Similarly, help from child guidance appears to protect young women at high risk from poor social integration. Those not receiving such help are at high risk of offending even though they are members of a generally low risk group in terms of their gender and social integration.

Who commits a serious offence?

It is more difficult to predict who will commit a serious crime after leaving specialised treatment centres. Although many young people are delinquent, few commit further grave offences so it becomes a problem of picking a needle out of a haystack. The most obvious place to begin looking is with those who had previously been convicted of crimes in the top five categories of the scale described in Chapter Four. But this proves unproductive as the following table shows. Focusing again on the same 170 young people, it can be seen that one in four of those who had never been convicted prior to a treatment sojourn commit a serious offence and that two-thirds of the 37 young who did so had committed one previously.

Table 8.3: Seriousness of offence committed before entry and after leaving specialised treatment settings

| | | AFTER TREATMENT | | | |
		Serious crime	Less serious crime	No crime	TOTAL
	Serious crime	24	46	40	110
Before treatment	Less serious crime	8	20	12	40
	No crime	5	7	8	20
	TOTAL	37	73	60	170

The data therefore resisted the logistic regression used in the previous section. But there are associations worth reporting here. The

CHAID analysis revealed that the most dangerous group are serious and persistent offenders who remain socially isolated on departure from the secure setting: just over half (56%) of them are convicted of crimes that top the scale of seriousness. The worst instances, thankfully very few, were rapists who showed little remorse for or insight into their crimes, who seemed likely to re-offend on release and did so. These young people had usually completed their sentence and so could not be kept in custody. Getting serious and persistent offenders into an orthodox social network clearly has some beneficial effect, as the following table shows.

Table 8.4: The proportion of young people in different sub-groups convicted of serious crimes within two years of leaving specialised treatment centres

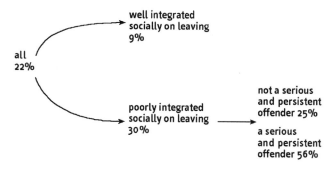

Difference in social integration is significant at the 95% level of confidence

Who goes home?

'Who goes home?' bellowed Members of Parliament across the chamber of the House of Commons in Victorian England. They were looking for company so that they would be protected from London street robbers. Here the question is more innocent. It is about predicting which of the graduates from specialised treatment centres goes back to live with relatives. This variable is selected since it indicates their ability to restore relationships with parents and other relatives which, in turn, is a reasonable indicator of employment prospects, ability to secure stable adult relationships and more, although these benefits can be offset by an increased likelihood of offending.

A young person was defined as having 'gone home' if he or she went to live with any relative who had provided shelter prior to the treatment sojourn. A successful reunion was said to occur when the young person wanted to go home and stayed for as long as he or she wished. For some this was just a few days but for most it was several months. Using these definitions it was found that three-fifths of the 170 leavers who were at liberty went home at some point during the two year follow-up. Thus, even these, the most damaged of young people, continue to use the resources of family members long after professionals have ceased their interventions.

In predicting who goes home, career route is the dominant variable. For example, nearly three-quarters (71%) of adolescent erupters and one-off serious offenders (77%) who had the opportunity to return did so, and four-fifths of young men in these groups were rehabilitated. Less likely to find a niche are long-term care order (45%) or special education cases (48%), although those placed for any duration in residential education settings - and finding stability - are exceptions within this wider group. Young women also appear tardy in reuniting with relatives, less than half (47%) going back within the two years compared with 64% of the young men.

A general outcome measure

These statistical explanations of outcomes are concluded with an all embracing measure. No one indicator is ever likely to give a satisfactory picture of a young person's situation but some proxy measures can be useful in unpicking underlying trends. For each of the leavers a judgement was made as to whether or not the young person was 'adjusted against wider social norms'. This evaluation was made by researchers based upon professionals' perspectives on the young person's living situations, social and anti-social behaviour, physical and psychological health, education and employment and dependency on state services for support. The measurement used as a baseline the young person's situation on entry to a Treatment Centre and not ordinary standards of child and adolescent development. Using this framework, two researchers and a consultant psychiatrist made an independent judgement on the young person's situation at two years. A score was then agreed, on a scale from very adjusted to extremely maladjusted.

To be consistent with the previous analyses results are again based on the 170 young people who lived in the community. It was found that just under half (46%) of leavers were found to be adjusted against wider social norms at two years. Once again, treatment regime appears as a possible explanatory factor but the vital ingredient is that the young person stayed for the full term so that the treatment was completed. Only 10% of those departing the centres prematurely were deemed to be adjusted after two years. Of those in the long-term care and special education career routes completing programmes described by professionals to be psycho-therapeutic, 59% were doing well two years on, against the 23% found for those finishing a behaviour modification regime, further suggesting an independent treatment effect. The extent of the young person's social integration was again significant although for this outcome measure deficits are offset by intelligence. This evidence is summarised in table 8.5.

Table 8.5: The proportion of young people in different sub-groups found to be adjusted against wider social norms two years after leaving specialised treatment centres

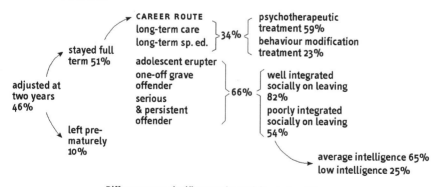

Differences are significant at the 95% level of confidence

Conclusion

Statistics can take us part of the way to explaining outcomes for extremely difficult and disturbed young people. It is clear that certain cases are more likely than others to offend, to commit serious crimes, to find a place back with relatives or gain some social adjustment. There seem to be predictable patterns and the findings should be useful to those dealing with difficult adolescents.

It is clear that career route, as described in preceding chapters, does influence outcome. It is also obvious, if disputable, that the type of treatment regime makes a difference and that staying the course matters as well as the method of intervention. There are specific effects within career routes; gender, living with parents and extent of social integration matter if young people's propensity to be re-convicted is being assessed. Much of this helps to clarify the individual predictions explored in subsequent chapters.

These findings also remind us how complicated are the underlying patterns. It is a nonsense to say that psycho-therapy is better than behaviour modification but in certain contexts for certain youngsters the type of treatment intervention does count. It would be erroneous to say that career explains all but there are clearly different outcomes for each of the five routes first outlined in Chapter Four. There are no simple solutions here but by exploring the way variables interact, some progress can be made. The diagrams used to illustrate the findings in this chapter make this point.

However we look at it, quantitative analysis can only take us so far. For example, for adjustment two years after leaving specialist interventions, it has been shown that three factors in combination are powerful predictors. A young person who stays full-term in a centre which attempts psycho-therapeutic treatment and who is on any of the career routes other than long-term state care is six times more likely to be adjusted two years on than had other conditions applied. Put like that the evidence seems overwhelming. But when checked against each individual in the study the prediction comes true in just 70% of cases; in nearly a third it is proved wrong.

So the findings here take explanations about outcome only part of the way. No matter how powerful the computer, how sophisticated the methods or how comprehensive the data, answers derived from statistics alone will always be deficient. Let us look at prediction another way.

9 Making individual predictions

Social researchers predominantly deal with groups and, as preceding chapters demonstrate, there are sufficient regularities to justify their faith in constructions like career route used throughout this book. But what is the best way of understanding the experiences of these young people - 204 individuals or five career routes? The problem is that while each young person is an individual, there are patterns in the way they behave. The methodological concern is to try and link the two, to build up a group picture from the individuals studied and from this to produce findings which might help professionals predict outcomes for a single case. The design of this study attempted to make such a connection.

The data outlined in Chapters Four, Six and Seven, together with some of the statistical evidence offered in the last chapter were used to predict the outcomes for 56 young people studied from the point of entry to the two specialist treatment centres. As previously explained, each case was dealt with individually and each prediction made was 'blind'. Outcomes two years after leaving were then compared with what had been forecast. Unlike the predictions discussed in the previous chapter which focused on a single indicator like conviction, this prognosis covered several inter-linked outcomes reflecting different areas of the young person's life.

These individual predictions were made in two ways. First, information on what was known from the retrospective study to happen to other young people on the five career routes was used to forecast what would happen to the 56 for whom outcomes were unknown. Second, the researchers worked in collaboration with a clinician; a consultant psychiatrist with long experience of work with difficult adolescents. He was able to help us recognise protective factors in the individual which reduced apparent risks, say of family breakdown, criminality and so forth.

These two strands of work and findings on their accuracy are described here; in the next chapter the results are used again to explain outcomes. First, let us look at the predictions about behaviour within or outside expected career routes.

Career

In Chapter Four, five career routes were established for the 204 young people studied. These have been used throughout subsequent parts of the book. To be clear about the coming analysis, it is necessary briefly to recap on the characteristics of the five groups.

First are the children long in state care; some of these are casualties of the system in that better care provided early on might have reduced the need for specialist services in mid-adolescence. The second career also comprises children long known to support agencies but by child guidance, psychiatric and psychological services, special education and occasionally residential mental health facilities as well as social services. Third are 'adolescent erupters' who have been sheltered by long-suffering relatives well into adolescence until their patience or staying power is exhausted and they ask social services to take a role. The fourth group also come late to the notice of welfare and control agencies but the explosion takes the form of a grave offence. Finally, there are young people who have been persistently delinquent in their early teenage years and who then graduated to more serious crime of a violent or sexual nature. If these young people can be described as having a conduct disorder, it is a disorder with many ingredients requiring treatment interventions on several fronts.

These five career routes were intended to be more than descriptive categories. It was hoped that they would have predictive powers, not just in one area but in all areas of the young person's life. For each grouping, a best outcome and a worst case result were set out. If the ideas were correct, the young people would stay within these limits for the duration of the follow up. In the Appendix the full details of the prognosis for each career route are set out; here, for the sake of brevity, a broad outline only is given.

Predicted outcomes for the five career routes

a) *Long-term state care.* As delinquency plays such a large part in the lives of young men in this group, and as persistent offending has such enduring negative consequences, different outcomes were predicted for young men and women. At best, it was hoped that the men would establish a relatively stable relationship, one which facilitates other orthodox social relations. Continuing insecurity and some minor delinquency was thought inevitable. Employment with aspirations for advancement would help but was thought unlikely. These men would eschew any social or welfare support.

At worst, property offending would continue to dictate future life chances; it would mean periods of custody, homelessness and fitful relationships. Dependency on alcohol or drugs was thought more likely and any legal employment less likely.

Similar patterns were expected for the women on this career route excepting that property offending would have diminished influence. At best a long-term relationship, frequently cemented by children which, in turn, improved relations with wider family members was predicted for women in the long-term care group, although such a *modus vivendi* would be fragile. At worst, there would be continued instability or adverse reactions to difficulties, with problems being presented to penal or health services.

b) *Long-term special education.* The most realistic forecast was of an inadequate person supported by others with similar problems. In contrast to long-term state care cases, these young people were thought more likely to use supports to amble from one minor crisis to another, particularly those with an identified learning disability. A stable relationship with a similarly insecure, inadequate partner would result in the 'best scenario'.

What of the converse? If the situation deteriorated, more movement was expected, at worst into contexts in which they clearly do not fit; for example, in prison standing apart from socialised delinquents. A vulnerability to manipulation, poor standards of hygiene and health and inadequate social skills are also part of the worst scenario for this group.

c) *Adolescent erupters.* At best, our assessment was for a fairly stable, independent person with some qualifications and settled employment. Relationships within the family home would still be tense and unease surrounding marriage or cohabitation expected. A minority were predicted to cut themselves off from parents to protect work situations and relationships.

The worst scenario was for a rootless youngster with a highly rejecting family. Continued delinquency of increasing sophistication such as credit card fraud and a failure to take employment opportunities were thought a likely consequence. Health difficulties associated with neglect and drug abuse and occasionally mental health problems were also included in the 'worst case' scenario for this group.

d) *One-off grave offenders.* Those one-off offenders who responded to treatment were expected to return home to relatives, pose no further offending risk, secure good qualifications and a settled job. Less promising was their social life; isolation and a failure to break away from the family in adulthood was part of the 'best case' scenario.

At worst, one-off grave offenders fail to admit guilt, engage in treatment or display remorse and will remain in prison custody. The stay in penal establishments will be long and movement between prisons common, thus weakening links with relatives. By virtue of their offence, sentence, age and length of stay, one-off offenders seldom have much in common with other prisoners. In the very worst cases, symptoms of previously latent mental illness requiring Special Hospital admission were predicted.

e) *Serious and persistent offenders.* At best independence, cohabitation or marriage was predicted. A lack of trust was thought likely to keep family relationships superficial but a probable counter balance was a wide social network, including a number of criminal friends. However, if all goes well there will be no serious crimes and no convictions. Finding jobs, occasionally in rather dubious circumstances, was also a part of the 'best scenario' for serious and persistent offenders.

The worst prognosis for young people on this career route is very poor indeed. Continued offending, some quite serious, would dictate all else; frequent sojourns in custody, poor family relationships, numerous criminal acquaintances but few, if any, close friends.

The success of predictions

The preceding cameos may be criticised for being too broad to be meaningful; but the research showed that professionals working with extremely difficult and disturbed youngsters often hope for much better or fear much worse outcomes than those just described. Whatever its weaknesses, the approach sets down markers against which the progress can be assessed.

When this method was applied to the 56 entrants to the treatment units, the following results were obtained.

Table 9.1: The number of young people within and outside predicted career route outcomes

| | OUTCOME | | |
Career	Within Predicted Bands	Out of Predicted Bands	TOTAL
Long-term care	11	3	14
Long-term special education	6	1	7
Adolescent erupter	6	1	7
One-off offender	16	0	16
Serious and persistent offender	12	0	12
TOTAL	51	5	56

As the table shows, when followed up, nearly all the young people remained within the career bands just described. Of the 56 against whom the predictions were tested, only five displayed life experiences which failed to match with the above scenarios. In two cases, mental illness not suspected in adolescence was diagnosed in adulthood. The first had been long in state care and was transferred direct from treatment centre to special hospital. The second had been known to child guidance and special education. Doubts about her mental health were raised during treatment. She left for a hostel, was later sectioned after several separate attacks on policemen and other authority figures and placed in a long-stay mental hospital.

The outcomes in the three remaining cases simply fell outside of that predicted above. Two of the three have been selected to illustrate the differences.

David

David was an 'adolescent erupter'. One of three children, he regularly attended school, performed well and posed no apparent difficulty until a few months before his 15th birthday when he was convicted of stealing a pensioner's handbag, an offence which propelled him into the orbit of social services. Meeting all the requirements of his supervision and intermediate treatment orders, David did well for ten months. However, he then made another unprovoked attack, pouncing on an elderly women from behind with a piece of cord. She fought him off and David ran away to school where he behaved as if nothing had happened.

His arrest was followed by placement in a local authority secure assessment centre. Here, the full scope of the crime was revealed; David had planned the attack for over two weeks and had been sexually aroused during the assault. The psychiatrist noted 'a cut off schizoid quality' in the offence and a place in a specialist treatment centre was swiftly secured.

Once there, further difficulties emerged. David had been sexually aroused by his sister undressing in their shared bedroom; the paternal grandfather was alcoholic and frequently disrupted their home life; there were other incidents of domestic violence and home was described as a 'cold house, nonetheless idealised by David'. Once away, David gained insights into these family dynamics. The specialist centre ensured a proper conclusion to his education, secured him a job in a restaurant where he excelled. The treatment also included sexual counselling.

On leaving, David completely cut himself off from home. He moved into a hostel where he met and soon after married a diagnosed schizophrenic. They set up home and, through his influence, she was able to maintain her medication and lead a reasonably stable life. They had a son and David secured a good job in a restaurant as assistant to the master chef. Nobody expressed any doubts about the success of David's progress and he did not commit any offences during the follow-up period.

In some respects David's behaviour was quite unlike that of similar youngsters; a stable marriage to a woman less fortunate than himself; the cutting off of parents and other relatives; the absence of any delinquency and the failure to excite unease in others about possible risk; the settling into a stable job which required considerable social skills and commitment - in each respect David's behaviour was markedly different from that of others who shared similar experiences.

Colin

Colin's childhood had been one of instability and unhappiness in state care. In adolescence he frequently ran away from children's and foster homes, regularly assaulted staff and twice attempted suicide. His file frequently refers to him being in 'moral danger' and 'a risk to other children': it later turned out that he is homosexual. In fact, Colin's main problem has been his experience of rejection; by his family, by the two schools which closed while he was a pupil, and by the countless foster parents and residential establishments which have said they could no longer cope. On top of this, there is a question mark about his mental health. At least two psychiatrists have noted the possibility of Asperger's Syndrome, a type of autism.

Colin was largely untouched by the specialist intervention experience. Neither could the specialist foster parent, who later assumed care, claim much progress, although their tolerance was admirable. Colin became a homosexual prostitute and built up a social network which took him abroad, including Amsterdam where he eventually settled in a middle class context. He is relatively affluent and personifies control. A professional would point his dependence to a series of transitory and possibly abusive relationships, something Colin would vehemently deny.

Sadly and almost inevitably, his downfall will be his health. His doctor treated him for having serious sexually transmitted disease and it seems only a matter of time before he is diagnosed as HIV positive. He never uses or expects a partner to use a condom.

In some respects, Colin's behaviour is much as we would expect for a boy long in state care. He has a series of unstable and dependent relationships, fleeting contacts with home, a delinquent lifestyle leading to poor health and no orthodox employment. But the context is entirely changed. The fact that he travels abroad, can mix easily with those of different classes and culture, is well off and apparently happy means that Colin has moved out of the bands that mark the edges of his stated career route.

Individual predictions

The second type of prediction concentrated not on groups or young people within their career bands but on what would happen to individuals. For each of the 56 young people entering two specialist centres, the research team worked with the consultant psychiatrist to predict what would happen during the stay in secure settings and during the two years after leaving. The predictions were once again blind; we had no way of knowing what would actually happen.

This is not the place to discuss at length the principles on which these predictions were based but the five areas which proved most useful to the team were inheritance: parental influences, other family factors including siblings' progress, life outside of the home, most notably peer and school relationships, and, finally, aspects of child development. As the following chapter demonstrates, in each of these areas there were risk and protective factors which influenced long-term outcomes.

Essentially, this analysis focused on the interaction of these risk and protective factors building on Rutter's observation in *Changing Youth in a Changing Society* that

> when two or more stresses occur together the risk goes up four-fold or more ....so that the combination of chronic stresses provides very much more than a summation of these separate stresses considered singly. (page 181)

An independent assessment of likely outcome was made for each young person. This was seldom precise; the prognosis included whether or not the young person would marry or cohabit but not to whom; it extended to the likelihood of getting work but did not say within which trade or profession; it dealt with future criminality and its seriousness but not the precise offence or its timing. The result was several pages in length but the following three examples of the summary paragraph written about each young person gives a flavour of the way in which the task was tackled.

Case A

> Highly dangerous. Will cause high anxiety to care staff. The staff in treatment centre will tell us whether this fear is a reality. High number of placements, he is unlikely to settle down either in treatment centre or later. Practically homeless - where is he

going to live? He won't hold down work - if he can get it. Don't expect much petty delinquency but could do something serious.

Case B

Not much has happened prior to the offence. If treatment centre can involve or get to know what is happening in the family he might settle on return. Clever - will do well in school. Attractive - people like him. Immature. Depressed. If we see this as a transient adolescent disorder, long-term outlook could be relatively good.

Case C

Outlook for future delinquency poor. People will expect something serious again. I think not a serious risk. She has committed a serious offence and people at home and in school have treated her pretty badly. Deviant family. Inconsistent fathering but warm relationship with mother. A reasonable capacity for feeling. A balance of risk and protective factors. With consistent care, a long-stay, a little bit of insight - she could do well.

The prognosis reflected not only what was known from the retrospective study and research on the risk and protective factors that affect these sorts of adolescents, but also the distinct features of each case. We referred earlier to the observations of the clinician on the special problems likely to face the young man whose mother worked in an Oxbridge college, sadly a forecast that proved accurate as the young man returned home, could not find work and, discouraged by his mother's disappointment, soon drifted into a drug sub-culture and the repeated pattern of instability that had characterised his life in state care.

Results of predictions about individual circumstance

Deciding whether these individual predictions were correct several years later was difficult. In some respects, the psychiatrist's observations were frighteningly accurate, as the previous example shows. But the aim was not to be precise. An independent researcher familiar with difficult adolescents was brought in to compare blind prognosis and outcome with the result that in 12 cases they were found to be significantly different. The greatest accuracy was achieved with the one-off and serious and persistent offender career categories. The adolescent erupters were the most likely to do something other than had been foretold, often doing much better than expected.

Table 9.2: The accuracy of individual predictions on entrants to specialised treatment centres by career route

Career	Prediction		
	Broadly accurate	Not accurate	TOTAL
Long-term state care	10	4	14
Long-term special education	5	2	7
Adolescent erupter	4	3	7
One-off offender	14	2	16
Serious and persistent offender	11	1	12
TOTAL	44	12	56

The 12 inaccurate predictions include the five cases who failed to stay within the career route bands described earlier. It will be recalled that these five included two where unforeseen mental illness developed and two who settled in contexts tolerant of their rather delinquent lifestyle. In the fifth case the young person's devotion to his sick wife produced a completely new set of living circumstances.

In six of the other seven cases, new information emerged during treatment which radically altered predicted and actual outcomes. For example, two girls disclosed child sexual abuse, shedding new light on family relationships, while in another case treatment staff discovered a long lost uncle who subsequently took in and gave employment to an otherwise 'homeless' leaver. In another case, researchers simply misinterpreted information in the case files.

Conclusion

What conclusions can be drawn from these findings? Above all else it should be said that there are underlying patterns to outcomes for difficult and disturbed young people, indeed for most other children in need, which should help strategic planning and work with individuals. Professionals have tended to resist such a possibility in recent years. Indeed, prediction when used in conjunction with labelling - the idea that by calling someone a delinquent they will become a delinquent - has become almost a dirty word in social work and its allied professions. A problem with the young people discussed in this book is that even a relatively small proportion of error causes anxiety and encourages caution. These political and pragmatic dimensions will always influence what actually happens to very difficult young people but exceptions should not detract us from the pursuit of accuracy. As we have explained, whilst we cannot say to whom somebody will get married or cohabit with, we can be reasonably sure about whether and when they will get married or cohabit and probably the social background of the person they live with. Admittedly, it is more difficult to predict with certainty whether the marriage will break down and virtually impossible to forecast the very small number that end in murder, but this does not diminish the value of prediction. The important point is to understand its limits and to use it appropriately.

The results also provide initial confirmation of the concept of career route first outlined in Chapter Four. The work with the psychiatrist also highlighted the importance of protective factors in modifying risk and therefore improving outcomes for children in need. This will be evident from the analysis described in the following chapter which brings together the qualitative assessments of outcome to explain why some extremely difficult and disturbed young people do better than others. This study started off a process of understanding which led to a body of subsequent research designed to explore how risk and protective factors interact to form chains of effects within career routes. If this explanation is successful, it should enhance the accuracy of prognosis and improve the planning available to those responsible for very difficult adolescents.

The prospect of all this research 'in the pipeline' might seem a doubtful blessing but, for now, the priority is to demonstrate the power of qualitative techniques in explaining outcomes.

10 Explaining outcomes

In Chapter Eight a series of statistical exercises were described. These began to explain why it is that some very difficult young people do better than others in adulthood. There are, in addition, three qualitative sources of information on which to draw. There is career route, the findings on who benefited from the treatment intervention and, emerging from the predictions on individuals just described, protective factors which mediate a risk. Obviously, there is some overlap with the statistical findings, particularly since the quantitative analysis also confirmed the place treatment interventions and career play in young people's life trajectories.

But the qualitative information works far better with individuals and therefore sits far more comfortably with clinicians, whether they be residential workers or psychologists. The finding that 50% of leavers are convicted within two years has to be important for strategic planning but professionals are bound to ask "will my case be in the half that gets into trouble or the half that doesn't?" What is more, clinicians have to be mindful of several outcomes; so it is not just the offending, it is the relationship with home, the chances of getting a job and so forth. In addition to this, they are less concerned with the precise outcome of, say, offending versus not offending than with knowing whether there is general improvement from the situation they found when they picked up the case - usually a very poor one for most of the young people discussed here. Ironically, this is essentially the value-added approach advocated by economists, which many social workers claim to eschew.

It will be recalled from the previous chapter that the predictions based on career involved setting out what would happen at best and at worst for each case in each of the five career route categories. It was found that all but five of the 56 followed up in this way stayed within defined bands, indicating that career as a concept has some explanatory power. But it does not explain what happens within the bands; why is it that some young people end up at the best end of the spectrum and others at the worst?

There are at least two possible answers. The first is that there are protective factors operating for certain individuals but not others. The second is that the treatment intervention has made a difference. It may, of course, be a combination or even interaction of the two. The data assembled on the 56 young people admitted to two treatment centres allowed us to test these possibilities.

As the following table shows, only five of the 56 had experiences not predicted within the career bands. Of the remaining 51, 24 came within the best outcome category, 12 at the worst end, leaving 15 in the middle. These outcomes certainly vary by career since those on the long-term state care route tended to bunch at the worst end of the spectrum and the serious and persistent offenders at the best. The questions are: first, do protective factors influence this distribution and, second, did the treatment intervention leave its mark?

Table 10.1: Outcomes for the five career routes

| Outcome | WITHIN CAREER | | | OUT OF CAREER | TOTAL |
	Best	Middle	Worst		
Long-term state care	2	4	5	3	14
Long-term special education	2	2	2	1	7
Adolescent erupter	3	3	0	1	7
One-off offender	12	2	2	0	16
Serious and persistent offender	5	4	3	0	12
TOTAL	24	15	12	5	56

Protective factors and career outcome

It is abundantly clear to many professionals that even the most difficult and disturbed young people are sometimes very resilient. But resilience is not something one has or does not have. Protective factors are not the converse of risk factors as, say, low intelligence could be put on the other side of a coin from high intelligence. An unusually high intelligence can protect certain young people in certain contexts but in other situations makes no difference whatsoever: some of the brightest people end up in prison, experience family breakdown and so forth.

The making of individual predictions with the clinical psychiatrist involved identifying potential protective factors and charting their interaction with possible stress points. Such patterns of interaction are best described in relation to real youngsters and two case studies follow later. First, it is necessary to set out the general areas in which protection was found.

Certain improvements came about as a result of the child's inborn constitution, cognition or identity. Whether the young person was extrovert or introvert, passive or overactive, clever or dull; in certain circumstances these attributes made a difference to the decisions they made. Those who were clever and used their intelligence as a focus for key life decisions were frequently shielded from the worst outcomes. Insight into personal histories, a distinction between past difficulty and future coping strategies and a desire to make life comfortable for oneself also helped. But even physical or social attractiveness can make a difference, for example, as happened in one probation officer's decision about whether or not to give an offender one more try. Such aspects of the individual and his or her personality improved the life chances of 10 of the 56 young people and were most influential in the case of one-off serious offenders.

For 11 of the 56 young people, the family or the young person's response to family difficulty provided a shield from the worst possibilities of the career. Frequently, better outcomes occurred because of the changed context in which the young person's problems were manifest. A recurring theme has been the way mothers' hostility to their daughters' choice of partners can moderate on the arrival of a grandchild. Certainly the perspectives of parents or other relatives were key when the young person was thrust into risky situations and particularly made a difference to the outcomes of those following the long-term care order route.

Family influences can take other forms. An underlying motive for the young person to behave, for example, to please family members or as a repayment for parental love, was evident in five of the 56 cases. The young person's ability to understand the continued shortcomings of his or her family and a recognition that guilt may rest with others make a difference. Continuing follow ups with this group are showing that parental control which is not undermined by alcohol, fatigue, drugs, parental discord or jealousy continues to be important, even when the 'child' is aged 25 or 30.

The way in which a young person interacts with the outside world also makes a difference to career outcomes; and was particularly evident in eight of the 56 young people, including two of the seven on long-term special education career routes. Fundamental strengths such as the sense of trust or stability or a reasonable level of self-esteem which can bolster against inevitable setbacks during early adulthood certainly build resistance but a simple desire to please or an ability to express and respond to affection also play their part.

Naturally, some young people benefit from several influences upon individual functioning. Overall, it was found that 21 of the 56 young people had their career prospects enhanced thanks to protective factors in personal functioning, family or other relationships. The following table shows that the adolescent erupters and one-off offenders were the most likely to benefit. It is also clear that protective factors are not a guarantee of best outcomes. Two young people, who had both been long in state care, did badly despite their resilient qualities.

Table 10.2: The influence of protective factors on outcomes for young people in five career bands

| | Protective Factors Operate | | | No Protective Factors | | | | |
	Best	Mid.	Worst	Best	Mid.	Worst	Out of Career	TOTAL
Long-term state care	1	2	2	1	2	3	3	14
Long-term special education	1	1	0	1	1	2	1	7
Adolescent erupter	1	2	0	2	1	0	1	7
One-off offender	7	1	0	5	1	2	0	16
Serious & persistent offender	2	1	0	3	3	3	0	12
TOTAL	12	7	2	12	8	10	5	56

To illustrate how protective factors can make the difference between a young person reaching the best as opposed to the worst possible outcome in his or her career route, two of the 56 cases are described. Both were chosen for inclusion because the contribution of the treatment intervention was benign and therefore had little bearing on outcome.

Elaine

By the time she reached her twelfth birthday, Elaine already had a long history of gynaecological infections. She had been sexually abused at home and after removal continued to place herself in potentially abusive situations. In the year prior to her placement in a specialist centre, psychiatrists worried about Elaine's future mental health. Depressed, delinquent and, at best, unhappy, there was a consensus that if she did not get help soon, serious and enduring problems would follow.

Our prognosis was dominated by the squalor of Elaine's home life and her subsequent instability. The family presented a facade of outrage at their ill-treatment at the hands of intrusive state agencies but even the most charitable assessment was sufficient to conclude that they had prostituted their daughter to over a dozen men. Elaine never stayed in one place for longer than eight weeks during her five years in state care. Towards the end of her 16th year, she was more often living rough and sleeping around than being safely placed.

Making a prediction required that we looked for positive qualities in the family relationships. Had mother ever shown any warmth to Elaine? Were mother's feelings towards Elaine any different from those for her other sons and daughters? To what extent had mother suffered similarly abusive relationships in her childhood? It was important to understand the context of the abuse and suggest whether Elaine might, despite considerable trauma, still have some ability to trust and relate to others in future adult relationships.

The family refused to engage in the treatment process but demanded their rights to regular contact. Elaine, slightly intimidated, talked little about past or current anxieties. She attended classes but never gained any particular skills or qualifications and participation in work experience programmes was little more than perfunctory. She did, however, stay in one place for 26 months and developed several enduring non-sexual relationships.

There was evidence that Elaine could be articulate and convincing in discussions with professionals. In some respects she had acquired these skills from her mother who used them to fend off social services. On leaving the treatment centre Elaine reversed the process and used the skills to get all the help she could. Moreover, she easily convinced a boy from outside her social circle that she had enjoyed a normal upbringing. They settled together and subsequently had a baby.

Elaine's situation two years after leaving treatment was the best that could be hoped for, given her background, and far better than had been anticipated. She was stable, happy, rather distant from the parental home, occasionally delinquent and a little pushy. She knew how to make her world secure and made deliberate and effective plans accordingly. She comes across as an intelligent, articulate and confident young woman; a presentation which could in one context make her vulnerable but in this context acts as a protective factor against instability, rejection and abuse.

Jasmal

Born in England, Jasmal spent the first five years of his life in Pakistan. By the time he went to secondary school, each of his four brothers had left home to start their own families. Communication with his parents was difficult, literally as well as emotionally. Jasmal spoke only English, his mother only Urdu. Even had they shared a language, it is unlikely that either would have found the words to understand Jasmal's crush on his English teacher.

While plans for an arranged marriage continued, Jasmal wrote love letters to the teacher. She did not reply. He started to telephone. She hung up. He started to wait outside her house until she drove to school. She reported the problem to the headmaster who arranged a meeting with Jasmal and his parents a few days later. The anxiety for Jasmal during the waiting period was unbearable. He took a kitchen knife intending to take his own life but, after several hours of vacillation, confronted the teacher and stabbed her six times in the arm and chest.

The teacher was rushed to hospital and only just survived. Jasmal was arrested, charged with causing grievous bodily harm and sentenced to five years detention. Therapy was tortuous. He responded instantly to the behaviour modification programme but gained little insight into the offence. His parents co-operated fully and communication was eased thanks to an Urdu speaking member of staff, but discussions never ranged to the aetiology of the offence.

The prognosis for Jasmal was, nonetheless, promising. His problem seemed to be that of establishing a personal and sexual identity in the context of confused cultural messages. His reaction was dangerously immature but once he had grown up a little and lived away from home, the likelihood of a repeat offence seemed remote. Moreover, Jasmal had two key protective factors operating on his behalf. Firstly, despite its inadequacies, the family was very close and the offence brought Jasmal's difficulties to the notice of his elder brothers who became determined to help. Secondly, part of his cultural inheritance was a desire to please the family: while lost under the weight of passion for the school teacher, it was re-established during the stay in treatment.

Jasmal served four years of his five year sentence. While in treatment he developed a crush on one of the female care workers but no further complications arose. Jasmal left to a hostel in his home area but was swiftly taken under the wing of his elder brothers' families. They found him work and, in time, he married, had a son and became reasonably successful in his brother's computer business.

Treatment intervention and career outcomes

In Chapter Five, several questions about the success of the treatment interventions were summarised by asking whether it:

a) fundamentally improved the young person's long-term prospects

b) helped but did not change those prospects

c) made very little difference, or

d) made matters worse?

Applied to the 56 young people discussed in this chapter, it was encouraging to discover that in no case did the placement reduce long-term opportunities. Given the sophistication, quality and expense of the intervention, this finding may appear trite or at least unsurprising. But given that many of these youngsters had previously suffered poor substitute care situations and, as the next chapter demonstrates, those in prison custody frequently deteriorate rapidly, it is an important finding.

Twenty one of the 56 young people emerged little changed by their treatment experience. In 16 cases the placement helped the young person's prospects in some way and, for the remaining 19, the intervention markedly improved the chances of a satisfactory re-integration into society.

These contributions by the specialist treatment centre appear to endure and influence outcomes. So, as the following table illustrates, 18 of the 19 graduates who were both changed and helped by the intervention had outcomes at the best end of the career spectrum while 11 of the 14 with the worst scenario were neither helped nor changed by the treatment experience.

Table 10.3: The contribution of the treatment intervention to outcomes within the career band

| | OUTCOME | | | |
Intervention	Best	Middle	Worst	TOTAL
Changed and helped	18	1	0	19
Helped but not changed	4	9	3	16
Neither helped nor changed	4	6	11	21
TOTAL	26	16	14	56

The contrasting way in which young people responded to the treatment intervention is now illustrated by two more of the 56 cases, Jack and Cathy. Both were selected because there was little evidence of protective factors operating on their behalf.

Jack

Jack's disturbance was evident within five years of birth. A referral to child guidance was followed by placement in a residential special school. Increasing patterns of violence and absconding led to several moves until he was taken into state care when he was fifteen. Continued delinquency and a potentially serious offence in which a stolen car was driven at a pedestrian precipitated the specialist placement.

The research prediction focused on several deficits which the intervention would have to address if success were to be achieved. Jack was born 10 weeks premature and weighed 2lbs at birth. His mother, concerned at the possibility of brain damage, was over protective, at best sheltering her fragile child and very probably failing to establish sufficient controls early on. Later family dynamics were highly disturbed; Jack was involved in indecent sexual behaviour with his older sister on several occasions during home leaves and he also defecated in his room.

In the residential context, relationships were hardly any better. Jack reacted badly to any firm structure or discipline. His delinquency took the form of gambling and sexual acting out with other boys within the schools - he was moved several times for buggery offences - and car theft on the outside. He had learning difficulties and few social skills.

The work of the treatment centre focused on each of these areas. Continuing EEG reports revealed minimal brain damage unlikely to affect functioning. High levels of contact with parents and some counselling work picked up on the deep-seated problems within the family and concluded with mother and son realising that they could not live peacefully with each other on Jack's release. A specialist foster family was found to look after Jack. They focused on his self-esteem and maintained firm boundaries; as his foster mother expressed it, they made him 'special within a context where all children in the family are special'.

A battery of skills training packages were used by the treatment centre. Most of these paid off although he was not a young person who responded easily to behaviour modification. The work experience programmes certainly encouraged him to develop normal social relations and introduced him to the world of work.

This intervention with psychotherapeutic and social learning dimensions targeted at specific deficits had its benefits. Two years after departure he married Marie, a woman who herself had had special educational needs as a child, and got on well with Marie's large and welcoming family. There were moments of stupidity. A few weeks prior to the final follow-up, he was hospitalised after jumping out of a second floor window while drunk at a party. But he was generally law-abiding, tried never to miss a day in his job stacking shelves at the local supermarket and was doing as well as could be expected for someone on the long-term special education career.

Cathy

Cathy received a life sentence after she murdered a 50-year-old man whom she accused of rape. Extremely delinquent in her mid-teens and a user of hard drugs, Cathy claimed to have been raped several times previously. Her accusations probably had some foundation but at least one psychiatrist dismissed them as fantasy, consequent upon a long history of sexual abuse.

Cathy was a serious and persistent offender for whom few protective factors could be found. The individual research assessment highlighted the lack of a close relationship with a parental figure. Cathy had been frequently separated during her early years from mother, father and step-parents, at least two of whom had sexually abused her. When at home she regularly witnessed abuse and violence. Mother had no feelings for her daughter and, when Cathy became sexually active in her early teens, she was also rejected by her two sisters and maternal grandparents.

After her 12th birthday Cathy never went to school for more than three consecutive days. She never formed a lasting relationship in secondary school and came to rely upon fleeting sexual acquaintances or drug pushers and users for friendship. The background, coupled with a very serious offence, did not bode well for the future.

The treatment centre concentrated on controlling Cathy's behaviour, trying to address her educational deficits and demonstrating to her the value of non-sexual relationships. In the first two areas progress was made. Cathy responded to the secure and controlling environment and clearly understood the system of rewards used in the treatment regime. She also did well in her studies passing two GCSEs and four RSAs. Cathy's social life improved. Frequent sexual relationships continued to be integral to her functioning.

The treatment for Cathy successfully targeted specific needs. The work did not address the roots of Cathy's disturbance which, by the research assessment, lay in infancy and early years - of never having bonded with a parental figure, in separation and abuse, and family dynamics - particularly her rejection by parents and siblings. In fact, although Cathy's mum was encouraged to visit, treatment staff never saw parents or siblings at any point during her four year stay.

Cathy was helped but certainly not changed by the treatment experience. She was moved on to prison where she remains. Psychiatrists, prison staff and social workers agree that she still has little insight into the murder and has great difficulty relating to other inmates and staff. She remains highly disruptive and refuses most opportunities to leave her cell, for example for classes or work experience. Cathy's outcome is very much at the worst end of that predicted by her career for a serious and persistent offender.

What influences a good outcome?

Why do some young people do better than others?   Describing outcomes is one thing but explaining them is quite another. Statistical analysis helps and shows beyond reasonable doubt that there are underlying patterns in the lives of extremely difficult youngsters, other children in need and, in all likelihood, all children. But statistics deal with groups, leaving the practitioner to struggle with the individual. They also tend to dwell on the single outcome - who offends, who goes home - while the clinician tries to link a series of outcomes to find a series of interventions that will make the best of a difficult job. The predictions made in this chapter are much closer to the professional task than those considered in Chapter Eight.

The starting point has been career, the interaction of life events, pathology and responses by welfare and control agencies which summarise much of what happens prior to a specialist intervention becoming necessary. There are few side avenues away from career routes: only five of the 56 young people studied have moved beyond the boundaries which define the five careers described. Knowing to which career group a young person belongs at 16 is therefore to know with a reasonable degree of accuracy what he or she will be doing at 21 or 25.

The problem with career is that the boundaries are wide. What separates a one-off offender who settles uneasily at home from another who remains in custody? What makes the difference between a reasonably acceptable outcome on any career route and the worst scenario for an individual?

Protective factors clearly help. Where individual prediction identified a protective mechanism and it came to operate during the two year follow-up, better outcomes frequently ensued. The treatment intervention also counts. Not so much the type of regime - although previous chapters have demonstrated this to be important - as the matching of intervention with identified needs. Where this happens, and change is achieved, better outcomes within the career range are more or less guaranteed.

How do protective factors and treatment interventions interact to influence a career outcome? As the following table demonstrates, where protective factors were present and the intervention both changed and helped the young person, the best of outcomes always followed. Turning this around; where no protection was apparent and the intervention neither helped nor changed the young person, the worst scenarios always came true. There are in between states. Twelve young people achieved the best outcomes thanks to the treatment intervention alone; for four it was the protective factors alone that made the difference.

Table 10.4: The influence of protective factors and treatment intervention on career outcomes

Career Outcomes	Protective Factors	Changed & helped	Helped but did not change	Neither helped nor changed	TOTAL
		Contribution of Treatment Programmes			
Best Outcomes	+ Factors	6	2	4	12
	No Protection	12	2	0	14
Middle	+ Factors	0	4	3	7
Outcomes	No Protection	1	5	3	9
Worst	+Factors	0	0	2	2
Outcomes	No Protection	0	3	9	12
TOTAL		19	16	21	56

Even a glance at these data should bring some encouragement to those who work with troubled children. Treatment makes a difference, even for those who entered with massive deficits. It also demonstrates that the failure of a specialised intervention is not a signal to abandon hope. Young people who will not respond to treatment or are moved prematurely sometimes make out; their natural resilience or other protective factors afforded by their personality or by their family will steer them to the friendly ports available on their career route. More work is needed to understand these influences on a child's life because there is probably much that can be done to enhance their power. For a group of people who have so little going for them, every little bit of help counts.

Conclusion

In this final analysis of the careers of young people leaving secure treatment units, an attempt has been made to explain the different outcomes found for individuals in each of the career route categories. The earlier analyses charted general patterns but these have now been explained. The fact that treatment experience and regime have been found to be important echoes the findings of research undertaken thirty years ago into approved schools, borstals and probation hostels; these studies established that regimes were important but were not sure why. By linking aggregated data on outcomes to treatment experiences and the characteristics of individual young people, it is hoped that this relationship has been clarified.

Treatment cannot be discussed without considering the needs of the young people, some of which are compensated by qualities in the young person. What actually happens to young people reflects an intervention between all these factors. The enduring message for service planners and professionals working with very difficult young people is that many of these patterns are predictable despite the idiosyncratic features of each case.

11 Outcomes from less intensive interventions

Early on, the placement options for extremely difficult and disturbed young people in the United Kingdom were outlined. The chapters that followed described the experiences and outcomes for those who received specialised help. What about those who get something less? This question is especially pertinent for countries that have never created highly intensive facilities for such youngsters or where, as in the United Kingdom, there has been something of a retreat from welfare approaches for those causing offence in society and a growing concern with cost.

Several research studies have sought to answer the question, 'what are the outcomes from less intensive interventions?' Two were undertaken as part of the project described in this book and their findings complement those of an authoritative review of the evidence on Section 53(2) cases by Ditchfield and Catan. Having scrutinised in detail the situation of 204 young people in highly specialised centres, this is obviously not the place to write at length about another set of outcomes. The findings of the research can be simply summarised - the more that is invested in a difficult youngster, the better the result tends to be.

In England and Wales, we estimated that there are, at any one time, between 110 and 150 young people meeting the criteria necessary for inclusion in this study. The number varies over time reflecting socio-demographic change. The following graph summarises the situation over the last 30 years and indicates the likely increase in volume over the next five.

Figure 11.1: The estimated number of YTC-type children in England and Wales between 1961 and 2001

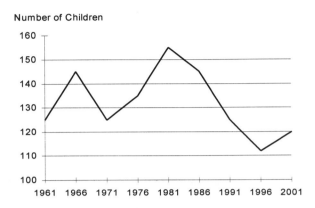

Number of Children

When this research began, seventy of these young people were allocated to the most specialised intervention available. Another ten per cent were in secure accommodation provided by local authority social services departments. These provided an intervention that was shorter, less sophisticated and less intense than that offered by the specialist centres. The remaining two fifths went into prison department young offender institutions where there was little in the way of treatment on offer although the training and education provision was often better than in welfare settings.

With changes in attitude toward difficult adolescents, the organisation of public sector services and planning of local authority secure accommodation, the number of highly specialised places has fallen in recent years. In compensation, there has been a commensurate increase in the availability of less intensive treatment facilities. What difference do these options make for a young person? Two case studies provide a contrast.

Karl

Karl was convicted of the indecent assault of a girl two years his junior. Karl was 15 at the time of the offence. He had four previous convictions for criminal damage, theft, burglary and robbery. He was sentenced to three years detention and placed in a local authority secure unit which sheltered seven other boys and girls. He had all the characteristics of other serious and persistent offenders described in this book.

The secure unit primarily focused on the management of Karl and three other serious offenders on the Unit, all young men. Karl was of especial concern because of the sexual nature of his offence. The remaining four residents, two young men and two young women were all in state care and had been placed in the unit because of the failure of local authority open settings to control them. Although all were very difficult, only Karl met the criteria that would have qualified him as a candidate for specialist help.

In the secure unit, the quality of care was very high and the remedial education was perfectly suited to Karl's needs. The treatment took the form of bi-weekly sessions with a clinical psychologist who focused on anger management, the establishment of ordinary sexual relations and understanding the motives for offending. There were no significant incidents during Karl's stay; in fact, for the most part he was obedient and quiescent. His mother visited once a month and promised him a bed when he left but there was little warmth in the relationship and hardly a pinhole of insight into how family circumstances could have contributed to Karl's offending.

Karl had expected to stay in the secure unit for six months prior to moving to prison department custody for a further six before release. In fact, his stay was extended to nine months in the local authority setting, with the remaining three in a young offender institution. Including remand prior to sentence, he served exactly half his allocated three years.

Karl returned home. As might be predicted he soon got back into trouble. He was cautioned for a burglary six weeks after release and then sentenced to nine months detention for an aggravated burglary three weeks later. Potentially, Karl poses a significant threat to women on his release.

Simon

Three weeks before his seventeenth birthday, Simon was arrested with three others for the unprovoked attack on and murder of a Pakistani boy four years his junior. Simon showed no remorse for the crime and was sentenced to indefinite detention. The psychiatrist's report was short and non-committal. Given Simon's age, it was unsurprising, therefore, for him to be sent to a young offender institution rather than to a treatment centre.

Simon joined a regime shared with 250 other young offenders; a small minority were serving longish sentences for serious crimes but the majority were in and out within a three month period. As a result, Simon quickly became an 'old lag' and, given his offence, one who maintained high status among the majority group of white men in the prison, not an auspicious environment to make progress towards successful rehabilitation.

Simon had a large cohesive family who visited reasonably regularly. But there was no part of the regime that allowed for their constructive involvement in Simon's development. In fact, over the four years we were in contact with him, Simon moved to eight establishments - some for a matter of days as part of a transfer - and family links became strained by simple geography.

Against that, Simon picked up five basic qualifications for trade skills like bricklaying and, when not excluded because of fights, attended remedial school classes. He was quite popular with prison officers in each of the prison establishments he lived in, particularly those which gave him an extended stay.

There were few criteria against which to gauge Simon's progress. He received a standard assessment from a psychiatrist each year as part of the Home Office review but, given the racial motive for the attack, there was little to interest the specialists. It became apparent a year after sentence that Simon would serve at least 10 years in prison establishments, depending on his behaviour inside. His very long term outcomes may be quite similar to other one-off serious offenders but it will be some time before we know.

To evaluate the effects of less intensive interventions, we charted over a two year period the subsequent careers of the 15 young people from the child-care secure units and young offender institutions who, as was seen in Chapter Three, qualified as 'highly probably' Youth Treatment Centre cases. We concentrated on two aspects of their careers, living situations and criminal histories, as both are reliable indicators of the overall capacities of problematic adolescents to function successfully in the community after release.

This exercise revealed that the situation of these young people during the two years following placement in a secure unit or young offenders institution very much reflected their situation on entry, a relationship which mirrors that found for leavers from the Youth Treatment Centres. Again, a career route perspective proved illuminating.

It will be recalled that our scrutiny of the characteristics of young people in the Youth Treatment Centres showed that the entrants fell into five distinct career groups. Applying the categories to the 15 'look-alikes', five were grave, one-off offenders. Of these, one who was detained at 'Her Majesty's Pleasure', moved straight from a long-stay local authority secure unit to prison and remained there for the two year follow-up period. Two others in similar accommodation were released home to parents and employment and neither got into further trouble during the next 24 months. The two who were in youth custody and who had been detained under Section 53 (1) of the *Children and Young Person's Act*, 1933 for murder, both served long prison sentences and did not offend after leaving.

Of the four young people in the serious and persistent offender category and placed in the long-term secure units, one, who was serving a life sentence for the rape of a young girl, moved straight to custody and remained in prison for the remainder of the follow-up period. The remaining three, each sentenced to four years detention, were released to the community and quickly got into further trouble. Two were sentenced to short periods of custody during the follow-up period.

Two other such cases in young offender institutions served extensive sentences before being released to the community. Neither committed a grave offence after leaving, although one was convicted of burglary and returned to custody. The second case was admitted to hospital on several occasions after attempting suicide but remained unconvicted two years after leaving prison.

Only one of 15 'look alikes' had been long known to special education, child guidance and psychiatric services before admission to security. Concerns that this young man was mentally ill could not be confirmed despite numerous assessments. However, when he indecently assaulted and caused grievous bodily harm to one of the kitchen staff in the secure unit, he was moved to a special hospital where he remained for the entire follow-up period.

The final three children had been sheltered from view by parents prior to an eruption of uncontrollable difficulties during mid-adolescence. One such boy who had been convicted of indecent assault later attacked a staff member in the secure unit, an offence which resulted in a 30 month youth custody sentence. He remained in a young offender institution throughout the follow-up scrutiny. The other two cases, one boy and one girl, resumed the patterns of difficult and disturbed behaviour once they had left. Neither was convicted but both were involved in prostitution and one became dependent upon heroin.

The outcomes for the 15 young people who received less intensive treatment are not surprising in the light of the evidence presented in this book and their pathology on entry to security. Many remain long in custody, reflecting continued unease about their potential for further crime. Those with long criminal histories continue to offend, although only a small number of them commit further serious crimes. Few remain out of trouble and none adopts the lifestyle we would hope for our own children. Nonetheless, given the poor prognoses on entry to secure accommodation or youth custody, these outcomes should be seen in context.

Given the few cases who qualified for inclusion in this follow-up scrutiny by virtue of meeting the criteria laid down for admission to a Youth Treatment Centre, it is difficult to make meaningful comparisons. We cannot simply compare reconviction rates of different institutions because the follow-up research suggests that the Youth Treatment Centres contain a significant proportion of young people who are both persistent offenders *and* very disturbed, a combination extremely rare in other secure settings. But what is clear is that there is no simple alternative that is outstandingly more effective; indeed, had the 15 look-alikes entered the specialist treatment centres, the follow-up evidence suggests that their outcomes would have been more favourable

This conclusion was reinforced by a different attempt to identify viable alternatives to secure treatment. There were six local authorities in England and Wales that had never (or very rarely) used long-stay treatment centres and the experiences of their very difficult adolescents might have indicated an alternative policy. The authorities were invited to nominate their most difficult cases over the past three years and proposed 30 candidates. There was an initial problem over defining what constituted difficulty as a long-term view tended to obscure the urgency associated with the acute crises that often preceded admissions to security. Young people came from similar backgrounds and had similar careers to the adolescents in the secure treatment centres, except there were more very delinquent (but not particularly dangerous) boys.

However, it was the combination rather than the presence of individual factors that proved significant. When characteristics were combined, as in the admission criteria used in this book, the numbers qualifying for 'look-alike' status fell to five, all of them young people who had experienced very turbulent careers indeed and had spent time in custody; moreover they moved around a lot in the period when they would otherwise have been in one treatment setting. There was no indication that the alternative experience conferred any benefit on them; their careers continued to display the frequent treatment breakdowns, ruptured and superficial social and family relationships, enduring criminality and sojourns in custody that long-term treatment seeks to reduce.

Outcomes

On whatever dimension considered, the outcomes for very difficult young people appear to reflect the time, sophistication and effort taken by the institution selected to intervene. So, on the simple measure of conviction within two years of departure, for example, outcomes are best from the specialist centres, next best from the medium intensive local authority settings, and worst from prison custody. These findings hold true even when young people's background characteristics, career route and protective factors are taken into account.

It has been seen that there is no certainty of 'cure' in the treatment offered in sophisticated settings. Nevertheless, those that remain outside generally fare worse. In the United Kingdom there are not sufficient specialist beds to take all of those most difficult adolescents. What would help, therefore, is a transfer of expertise from one setting to another so that young people in small, less extensively resourced units or in prison custody for a lengthy period get some opportunity to develop their best potential.

12 Conclusions

There are young people like those described in this book in every economically developed nation. While more can always be done to prevent problems accumulating to the point that highly specialised, secure facilities are necessary, there will always be youngsters such as these. Every 15 years or so a Mary Bell or Jon Venables; every month, another young murderer who does not attract notoriety; every week other youngsters whose needs are more complex, too complex some would say for journalists or the public to understand. These young people, who number no more than 150 in each year in England and Wales, form the tiny tip of the iceberg of 600,000 children in need, half of whom get some form of help from the personal social services.

Very few countries invest in research to find out who these young people are, what is done to help them, what kinds of specific interventions make a difference, what happens in the long run and, most importantly, why it is that some do better than others. The evidence is instructive. It tells us a little about how to prevent problems arising in the first place; it tells us much more about how to improve services for difficult adolescents generally and it tells us most about how and when to intervene and where to invest the greatest proportion of resources. If we can get it right with these youngsters - and the research would suggest that often we can - then we should be able to get it right with those posing lesser difficulty.

The book draws to a close with summary observations on the young people, the process of dealing with difficult adolescents, the nature of available specialist interventions, the lessons for research and, the primary purpose of all this endeavour, outcomes - what works, for whom, when and why. Interspersed throughout are single line cameos of the case studies appearing throughout the book; a reminder to us all that the people being discussed actually exist.

The young people

Strict criteria were established for inclusion in the study. By the standards applied in most developed countries, those coming under the research gaze have been defined as extremely difficult. Only in the United States, where a greater availability of drugs and guns increases the incidence of homicide committed by adolescents who elsewhere would be more orthodox delinquents, will some adaptation be necessary.

The 150 or so who come to notice in England and Wales attract some local notoriety either by virtue of their crime - murder, arson, rape - or the cost of the intervention required to maintain stability - often ten times the price of the most expensive private boarding school. Once a decade, one of the youngsters will attract attention across the Western world. What is surprising is how uninterested people are in between times; or how little media coverage is devoted to the more complex cases who have fallen out with relatives, have few friends, will not go to school, suffer an obscure health problem and have committed a grave crime. Maybe these youngsters frighten us with their complex needs and make us feel guilty for letting them down.

The complexity of their needs is at first mind-boggling. To start with, we know so much more about these young people than any other children in need. Seemingly, every profession takes an interest in them and the files rapidly expand. Every page explores another risk factor which interacts with one appearing in the previous section only to be ameliorated by a potential protective mechanism highlighted by somebody else. Each case takes professionals to the limits of their understanding and is usually beyond the ken of the typical lay person. No wonder the media take shelter behind words like 'evil'.

But there is an underlying pattern to all this misery. That much is evident in the young people's careers, the interaction of the decisions they make (or family and friends make on their behalf) and those made by the professionals charged to meet their needs. Career, defined in this way, appears to predict much about life chances. Five groups have been identified: those young people long in local authority state care who become beyond the capabilities of good open provision; those long dealt with by education, school psychology services and mental health; those adolescents previously unknown to control and welfare agencies whose behaviour deteriorates in mid-adolescence; those who commit a one-off grave crime; and persistent delinquents who commit a serious offence.

The term 'career' has been used in several previous Dartington studies and other child-care research. What is its relevance to people working with difficult adolescents?

The research has shown that there is some order and pattern to the referrals to specialist units. Observers may argue with the categories and it would probably be impossible to get agreement over the labels, but only those determined to see every case as different would disagree that there are common features within the five groups and that there are features that make each category distinctive. Two tests have been applied to convince the reader of the validity of the career groups. First, researchers and a clinician allocated the cases independently of each other and came up with broadly the same results. Second, the young people's background characteristics were analysed, using cluster and discriminant statistical analyses. The categories stood up to both tests.

Even this would be simply of limited interest if the groups had no predictive qualities. But, within a reasonable degree of confidence, it is possible to say what a long-term state care case or an adolescent erupter will be doing two years after referral, five years on et cetera. There is some indication of where they will be living; what kinds of family and social relationships they will enjoy; how much trouble they will get into; whether they will go to school, get a job, fall ill or move about and the same would be true for other groups of difficult young people.

In this context, this evidence should improve our knowledge about whom to intervene with (it is unlikely that all cases will receive or could benefit from the most specialised help), how precisely we should fashion the intervention (both at the time of crisis and in the long-term) and how we can measure the effects of our efforts. Twenty-five years ago it was enough to build new facilities, fill them with experienced staff and refer those young people whom nobody else could handle. Putting males and females together was the radical breakthrough in 1971. Today we know more, should be able to achieve better results and know when we have achieved them.

The process

Pattern and order are less apparent in the response of the State to these young people. To say the process is complex would be charitable. To say it is messy would be coming closer to the truth. Mess may not be a bad thing when dealing with adolescents, especially where flexibility and adaptability follow but successive additions to legislation, national policy, local services and provider organisations has made the system very difficult to understand. The exclusion of young offenders from the reforms which led to the *Children Act*, 1989 did not help. The summary in Chapter Two is as good an overview as will be found for England and Wales but it is probably already out of date. Some consolidation will be necessary if each player in the process is to comprehend fully his or her role in relation to others.

This is not to say that current arrangements are without strengths. For many of the young people who are the subject of this book, the process produces results. The pragmatic English make it work but the system does not have its own internal logic. If we were starting from scratch, could we say with any certainty that the process we would design would look much like anything currently in place? What would we seek to change?

Since the implementation of the *Children Act*, 1989, child welfare in England and Wales has become increasingly a needs-led service; it is moving away from being driven by available provision. In this, secure accommodation and services for the most difficult and disturbed young people have moved much more slowly than other parts of children's services. Too often, the number of beds has determined the threshold defining extremely difficult or disturbed when it is the threshold that should determine the number of beds.

Increasingly - again using England and Wales as a benchmark - services are designed to meet the identified wide-ranging needs of children and young people referred for help. Once known to health, education and social services, most cases behave predictably and this information can be used to design an effective response to children's problems. Too often the young people described in this book have been marginal to available interventions and the 'specialism' of the specialist places is their ability to pick up the pieces.

All this adds up to a failure to apply concepts that characterise a modern child welfare service to the most difficult cases. Much has been written about linking the concepts of need, threshold, services and outcome and some research teams have worked closely with local authorities to put these ideas into practice. The aim has been to move child welfare agencies on from offering isolated initiatives to ones which prioritise risk, introduce eligibility criteria, encourage practitioners to respond creatively to the needs of children and families and adopt a perspective that sees all services as integral to a continuum, each part of which is useful to different cases at different moments in their care careers. All of this has become commonplace in the child protection arena but it is hardly entertained when it comes to very problematic adolescents. The end result is a piecemeal design which is no longer sufficient for the complexities it is intended to address.

Intervention

The last stop for the youngsters, as far as child welfare is concerned, is a handful of specialist treatment centres. The commitment of staff within these places has to be unceasing if progress is to be made. But there is a balance to be found. Attention lavished on the world inside the treatment centre can detract from the requirements imposed by those outside who must pay for, regulate and monitor these places. During the time this research has been undertaken, specialist treatment centres have closed because of malpractice by staff, who cared much for the residents but paid little attention to the expectations of residents' families, social workers and funding agencies; and some would claim that humdrum places that have served the needs of external agents well have remained unchanged for too long.

The publication, *Structure and Culture in Children's Homes* discusses the benefits of organising a residential centre so that the societal goals, formal goals and managers' belief goals accord with one another. Much of this is relevant to the organisation of specialist centres for very difficult young people especially since concordance can lead to healthy staff and child cultures within residential centres, a vital ingredient in the success of secure settings. These cultures in turn lead to contexts which are generally acknowledged to be 'good', which in turn achieve positive outcomes for children and families.

Whilst this approach offers a promising model for beneficial change, what is missing is any reference to regime, yet the results suggest that regime is pivotal. This study shows that when working with extremely difficult and disturbed young people, the nature of the regime is especially important, probably because the centres are much larger and more sophisticated than the average children's home and the young people stay longer. In working towards the establishment of 'good institutions', regime has to be considered in addition to questions about achieving concordance between structure and culture. Although the best specialist centres visited as part of the research differed in their overarching ethos and underlying principles, at least as far as these are expressed in documentation, in day to day practice the contrast was more of degree than type, so there is a lot of common ground.

The disclaimer 'at least as far as these are expressed in documentation' is added because of a failure of specialised treatment centres both here and abroad simply to describe what they do. Behaviourists deserve less reproach than psychotherapists but both have tended to hide their strengths in the cloak of barely intelligible terms more concerned with process than outcomes. The descriptions of differing approaches contained in Chapter Five are barely adequate but at least they represent an attempt to summarise in plain terms what the treatment centres are trying to achieve. Much more of this, ideally written by practitioners, would be welcome.

As well as explaining the sophistications of therapy, such descriptions might also extend to the practical help and support that makes the difference between a successful and a very successful intervention. For knowing where a young person will live, how they will get on with family and friends, how they will cope with intermittent health crises and ensuring that they fulfil their educational potential or get a job is as important as gaining some insight into an offence or previously failed relationships. If the nature of the task is as wide as that suggested here, it goes without saying that the help of several agencies will be required; that the treatment centre cannot do the job alone.

This 'whole child' perspective goes hand in hand with a requirement to think long-term and of matching interventions with needs. There are clearly benefits of psychotherapeutic interventions for some young people at certain moments in time; for others, at different moments, behaviour modification techniques should be preferred. It is easy to forget how much a young person changes between 15 - the typical age of referral to one of these specialist centres - and 18 - the typical age of departure. The skill required of professionals is to marry the process, as it is defined in this book, with the life route, so achieving the best possible outcome within a career band; and to attempt to maintain the match throughout and beyond the treatment intervention.

Messages for research

This book has tried to build on previous studies in this field. For those familiar with Dartington's work, much of the approach will be familiar: the mixing of quantitative and qualitative techniques which ensures confidence in results that comes from large samples and insights into individual cases gained from an intensive look; the longitudinal perspective, following young people and their families over time; the interest in outcomes, what works, for whom, when and why; the determination to look at the whole child and not just the principal reasons for referral and the use of the terms 'career' and 'process'. But the book also marks a departure in that it seeks to explain outcomes, and therefore bring some additional rigour to the 'what works' debate. It is the first time we have fully defined the terms 'life route', 'process' and 'career' and attempted to show how they are linked. The hope is that this will contribute to the achievement of a common language in child welfare research; so that when similar studies are mounted in Newcastle, New York or Nuremberg, researchers can have a surer sense that they are comparing like with like. Clearly defined and widely accepted concepts move child-care research a little further forward towards a unified theory of children in need.

What does 'a unified theory of children in need' mean? 'Unified' refers to two types of connection; first between the concepts, methods and approaches, such as career, process, life route, risk indicators and protective factors, and second, between the ideas that underpin research, the organisation of the personal social services and professional practice.

'Theory' also refers to concepts which help predict. The hope is to be able to say if one does research in a particular way, it will produce a specific type of evidence; if one organises personal social services according to the same ideas, a particular pattern of services and outcomes will follow; if one applies the concepts to an individual case, better results with children and families will be achieved. By calling this 'a theory of children in need', the claim is that groups of children can be defined that have discrete experiences and warrant specialist research, a specified set of services and a consistent professional response.

All of this represents a tall order and the image may, in retrospect, turn out to be little more than a chimera. The most contentious aspect is prediction. But however much the reader may quarrel with the findings, it would be hard to dispute that for most young people studied there have been clear links between experiences prior to, during and after their stay in treatment. Would it not be beneficial, given the evidence discussed, if there were some place for the methods used in identifying these predictabilities in the organisation of personal social services and in individual practice?

Let us be clear about what this means. We cannot say which ten of the several hundred thousand children in need each year will be convicted of a homicide. But we ought to be better than we are at predicting which 5,000 of the 30,000 children looked after each year will stay long away from home and be vulnerable to 'drift'. And we can be reasonably certain about the prospects of the 150 or so among the 5,000 long known to child welfare agencies whose situation requires specialist interventions.

Outcomes

The most important part of this study is outcome. Inevitably with such a group of young people, there are some shock and horror stories. As we have recorded, four of the 204 have died since leaving the centres, two have been convicted of murder and are locked up for life, eight have developed serious mental health problems that have necessitated placement in secure special hospitals and another five have committed serious sex offences. For ten per cent of the leavers, therefore, it does not matter how one analyses outcome, the results are less than edifying.

There are also picture book successes worthy of the glossiest magazine. The 16 year old with a tortured childhood who found steady work and managed to support his schizophrenic wife and his son; the young people who returned to live with relatives they had tried to murder. For every sensational disaster there has been a sensational success. But for the great majority of the 204 young people, the outcome has fallen somewhere between these extremes.

Perhaps the most disappointing results have been to do with outputs; that is to say measures of professional activity. The contrast between what these young people receive in specialist treatment centres and what they get after leaving is frequently sharp. Local authorities are capable of investing several hundreds of thousands of pounds on a long-term state care case up to the age of 18 years but often do very little thereafter, even to the extent of refusing to allocate a social worker. Prediction ought to extend to a reasonable sense of how much expenditure will be required from point of referral to achieve a reasonable outcome at 21 or, better still, 25 years.

There is also a contrast to be drawn between the progress made by the young people and development within their families. On the whole, the young people move on but their families do not and nor is there much change in the environment in which the young person lives. More could be done to draw relatives into the treatment process and to link institutional and community intervention while the young person is away. At the every least, this finding is a reminder that treatment should teach strategies to help the young person cope with what has contributed to their difficulty in the past.

These messages are particularly important since most young people return home at some point to live with relatives and most of those who fail to get back have some contact with their family. There may be a continuing reliance on birth family since, on the whole, extremely difficult and disturbed adolescents are not good at making enduring relationships, although five per cent of those followed up got married within two years and ten per cent became parents themselves.

The finding that the environment to which young people return remains depressingly constant is a reminder of the importance of education and employment opportunities to those who are disadvantaged. Yet, on the whole, attention to social functioning has been allowed to detract from attention to education so that, despite extended stays, few graduates from specialised treatment emerge with useful qualifications; and the consequence of that is that two-fifths never find work and half of those who do get employment lose it quickly because they do not have the wherewithal to cope with the ordinary stresses of the work environment. That just eight of the 204 leavers found skilled work of any kind is an indictment of professional attitudes to education and employment for difficult and disturbed young people.

In other areas, where efforts have been more concentrated, outcomes are more encouraging. The physical and psychological health of graduates is reasonable, given the poor expectations on entry to treatment. Their pattern of living arrangements usually reflects the pattern established prior to the treatment sojourn, which is a problem for those long in state care but reasonably auspicious for those who are not. Offending outcomes are also positive. Naturally, the goal has to be no repeat serious offending, an objective not yet met. But, generally, conviction rates were lower than had been expected and for the first time in many years of working in this area, the prospect of a relationship between different treatment strategies and improved offending behaviour was apparent.

In the end, outcomes reflect three aspects of the study. First, the career route along which the young person has travelled prior to moving into a specialist centre; this sets out within broad parameters where the young person will live, with whom, how they will get on with family, what sort of job they will get and so on. Second, the nature, quality and matching of treatment intervention with identified needs; these make the difference between a young person reaching his or her full potential within a career band or drifting towards the worst end of the outcome spectrum. Third, the existence of protective factors; these make a difference to the extent that, in a handful of cases, a failed treatment programme can be offset by some individual strengths in the young person which see him or her through.

Endpiece

While stressing that outcomes are moderately good and predictable, we would conclude with a note of caution. The study has made us aware that a positive situation at 18 or 21 is no indication of a life happy thereafter. Many have stored up problems of health or of isolation from work which will haunt them later on. Many have settled in happy domestic relationships which are supportive now but will come under strain in subsequent years. Most of the grave offenders have been law abiding but must be considered a risk well into their 30s.

The relative absence of scientific and practice knowledge about what happens to children in need between, say, the ages of 18 and 25 or 30 is striking. In the past, researchers and professionals have tended to approach young adults as being meely extensions of young people. So, we complain about a task remaining unfinished (like the failure to offer a good education) but are little concerned with a new task (like encouraging late entry to continuing education or teaching social skills to stay in work). Working with young adults is not about doing more of the same.

So, like much research, this study has spawned further explanation. At Dartington this means continuing the follow up of the young people described in this book. We want to know how careers develop, whether or not protective factors continue to operate and how long the effects of treatment last. It is, after all, only by looking at what happens in the very long-term that we can know whether the cautious optimism that has been a feature of this book is, in fact, well founded.

Appendix 1

Presenting the best and worst scenarios in each outcome area for the five career routes

In the body of the text, we summarised the best and worst outcomes predicted for the young people on each of the career routes. As we expected the situation of long-term care order boys to differ from that of girls, we gave them separate prognoses. We used evidence from the retrospective study and from other research on difficult adolescents' transitions to adulthood to predict what would happen in each of the outcome areas under scrutiny. So, we estimated the best and worst possibilities in the areas of; living situations; family and social relationships; physical and psychiatric health; social and anti-social behaviour; education and employment and dependency on statutory services. As it was impossible to cover all possibilities, we also stated the likely exceptions to our prognoses, that is to say, those who would defy our predictions.

We hypothesised that, in the long-term, the young people would remain within the best and worst bands we describe. For each young person we made the prediction at the point of departure from the Youth Treatment Centre and looked again two years later to see whether or not we were accurate. The assessment was made by two researchers looking at the case independently and was checked by other advisors including the consultant psychiatrist working with the team.

We cannot fully describe all the criteria used in constructing the prognoses or for evaluating the outcome. However, the following details give a flavour of the method and are sufficient for readers to judge the rigour of the test. At first sight, it might be considered difficult for a young person's progress to fall outside of the bands described. However, it will be recognised that, when all the outcome avenues are combined the boundaries are, in fact, tightly drawn. We found that a young person doing well in one outcome area, for example living situations, also tended to enjoy good progress in the others. Similarly, a collapse in one area, such as social and anti-social behaviour, also heralded difficulties in other areas of the young person's life.

Career route 1: Long-term care order

(a) Males

Outcome Area	Best	Worst
Living Situations	Cohabiting, possibly married. Subject has dependency on these relationships including any children.	Unstable, moving between short-term relationships. Occasionally homeless and imprisoned.
Family and Social Relationships	Insecurity will mean a small network outside of family.. Weak on support but not on social life.	Isolated loner or linked into a drug or delinquent sub-culture. Superficial relationships.
Health	Good physical and psychological health.	Poor mental health and physical health problems consequent on drug abuse and living situations.
Social and Anti-social Behaviour	Minor delinquency (Black market). Polite. Aspirant.	Persistently delinquent.
Education and Employment	Little education but stable employment and quietly aspirant.	No legal employment. No education outside prison.
Dependency	None. Avoids dependency.	Very dependent and resists attempts to help.
LIKELY EXCEPTIONS	Those finding a niche in middle-class sub-cultures.	

(b) Females

Outcome Area	Best	Worst
Living Situations	Married, children. Stable. Young person in charge of home.	Caught between mental health and custody. Typically 'Holloway' Prison. Unsatisfactory existence in community. Prostituting. Abused.
Family and Social Relationships	Stays in touch for sake of grand-children but young person-parent relations remain cool.	Rejected by family and young person rejects some of her own children.
Health	Normal.	Poor mental and physical health characterised by depression and manifest in self-mutilation. Poor hygiene and sexually transmitted disease likely.
Social and Anti-social Behaviour	Some shop-lifting, black-market activity, defrauds social security.	Delinquency a symptom of mental health problems.
Education and Employment	None	None.
Dependency	Health and social services have concerns about any children but otherwise little dependency.	Highly dependent; unable to cope for extended periods in community.

Career route 2: Long-term special education

Outcome Area	Best	Worst
Living Situations	With parents, stable within an inadequate family setting.	Not great movement but living situations (hostel, sheltered housing) tend to be of very poor quality.
Family and Social Relationships	Likeable. Possibly married to a similar person. High contact with family.	Lost touch with home and falls in the wrong crowd, eg persistent delinquents. Taken advantage of.
Health	Accident prone. Out-patient at hospital.	Failure to look after him/herself (eg poor diet). Professionals frequently speculate on possible organic problems.
Social and Anti-social Behaviour	No delinquency.	Silly offences, delinquency to survive or attract attention. Behaviour frequently out of context eg sexual behaviour.
Education and Employment	No education but menial, stable work.	None.
Dependency	Social services and other welfare agencies take benign caring role.	Very dependent but agencies have no solution and the case is passed around between them.
LIKELY EXCEPTIONS	May be excluded from work in areas of high unemployment.	

Career route 3: Adolescent erupters

Outcome Area	Best	Worst
Living Situations	Independent and stable.	Continuing instability including some periods of custody.
Family and Social Relationships	Contact with relatives but overall quality of relationships poor.	Rootless, cut-off from a rejecting family.
Health	Very good physical and psychological health.	Ill-health associated with poor self care and drug use.
Social and Anti-social Behaviour	No delinquency. A small network of friends outside of family. Causes unease in both family and friends.	Delinquent and potentially dangerous. Offences wide ranging to include fraud. Attention seeking acting out.
Education and Employment	Some qualifications, in stable employment and aspirant.	Cannot hold down work. Aggressive in work situations.
Dependency	None.	High dependency on mental health, custodial and social services (especially the women).
LIKELY EXCEPTIONS	1) Family relations are restored by the treatment experience. 2) Young person cuts him/herself off from family in order to succeed.	Women having a lot of children but allowing them to enter care or accommodation in first years of life.

Career route 4: Serious one-off offender

Outcome Area	Best	Worst
Living Situations	With relatives and stable.	In custody and regularly moved.
Family and Social Relationships	Some relations outside of the immediate family network.	Social isolate.
Health	No health problems.	At least disturbance and possibly mental illness.
Social and Anti-social Behaviour	Has resolved problems that led to offence. No delinquency.	Causes anxiety and is delinquent in custody.
Education and Employment	Gets qualifications and skilled work.	Refuses education and employment in prison.
Dependency	On licence but otherwise none.	High dependency on prison services, probation and health.
LIKELY EXCEPTIONS	Girls getting married and having children of their own.	Severe mental illness necessitating removal to special hospital.

Career route 5: Serious and persistent offenders

Outcome Area	Best	Worst
Living Situations	Independent, occasionally cohabiting.	Periods of homelessness and custody. Frequent movement.
Family and Social Relationships	Large social network including some delinquent friends. Contact with parents secondary to this.	Abusive to family but remains in contact. Lots of acquaintances but no friends.
Health	Heavy drinking, some drug use.	Undernourishment linked to excessive drug use.
Social and Anti-social Behaviour	Some minor delinquency but never convicted.	Offending, either potentially or actually dangerous.
Education and Employment	Always working but movement and non-legitimate employment.	No work. Not bothered.
Dependency	None.	Low but professionals wish it were higher. Unrewarding work.
LIKELY EXCEPTIONS		Persistent rapists.

Appendix 2

References

There has been a conscious decision not to clutter the text of this book with references. The literature on secure units is fairly sparse and residential child care has been well served by literature reviews. Publications on treatment, in contrast, are extensive and there is an international audience, hence it was felt that constant citations would interrupt the flow for the reader.

An overview of residential child care is provided in Bullock, Little and Millham, *Residential Care for Children: A Review of the Research*, published by HMSO in 1993. This discusses common findings from 117 studies but it is significant that only four of these focus on secure units. More recent studies and others that were regarded as too specific for inclusion are listed below.

Secure accommodation for children has long been a contentious issue but the numbers affected at any one time have varied considerably. In the two decades after the Second World War, security for offenders was provided in borstals and detention centres but some 10,000 delinquents were sent to approved schools which were open establishments run on boarding school lines. In the 1970s, several studies were commissioned to explore the effects of different regimes on young people's behaviour. Reports from Dartington (Millham and colleagues), The Home Office Research Unit (Dunlop, Cornish and Clarke) sought to identify patterns and similar results emerged from studies of other residential settings, such as probation hostels (Sinclair) and Borstals (Bottoms and McClintock).

The treatment of disordered adolescents in secure accommodation did not become an issue until the mid 1960s when three closed units were built on approved school sites. These were evaluated in *Locking Up*

Children (Millham et al., 1978) and by practitioners, such as Hoghughi. There were similar studies of the newly established Youth Treatment Centres by Cawson and Martell, Martin and Lawes.

In the 1980s, interest shifted from the effects of regimes to the processes by which young people arrived in secure accommodation and their experiences while there. Studies exploring these issues were undertaken by Harris and Timms, Kelly, Petrie and Stewart and Tutt. Thereafter, interest waned somewhat and most child care research in the 1990s has focused on child protection. Although there has been renewed activity in the field of adolescent mental health, recent research has tended to focus on specific types of treatment or on groups with particular needs, such as young women, violent offenders or abuse perpetrators. Compared with the legal, policy and economic concerns raised by secure units, research interest in what happens to the young people has been relatively sparse.

Studies of residential institutions and career routes

This study of the care careers of young people in Youth Treatment Centres and other specialised provision is one in a series of Dartington studies beginning in the 1960s with research into boarding schools. A methodology with which to analyse the structure and processes of residential settings was published in *A Manual to the Sociology of the School* (Lambert et al., 1970). This sought to combine structural/functional perspectives on institutions developed by Etzioni and, somewhat more dramatically, by Goffman, with the ethno-methodological and interactionist explorations of Polsky, Becker and Coleman. This approach informed a study of approved schools, *After Grace-Teeth*, which compared 18 establishments and followed up 1,138 boys for two years after leaving. The next area of interest was secure units but, as explained, the focus of concern had shifted from regimes to the processes that led to admission and the various options available along the way. Nevertheless, a similar follow-up of leavers was undertaken and published in *Locking Up Children*. This continuing research interest led to the present study.

Since the implementation of the *Children Act*, 1989, residential care has been viewed in the wider context of services available to children in need; thus its relationship with other provision has increasingly been of interest. While this has been illuminating for understanding what happens to most adolescents referred to social services, it has not provided much new information on secure units as they only shelter a tiny proportion of all those looked after. The Dartington Unit has, however, attempted to keep traditions going with studies of a therapeutic community, *A Life without Problems* (Little and Kelly), and *Young Men in Prison* (Little).

The intellectual reference points in this research history are worth recording. We take from the early studies of structure and process two perspectives: the importance of the links between the various components of residential settings and the impact that regimes can have while the young people are there. The research approach has always been empirical and positivist, although we remain somewhat sceptical about questions of inference and proof. It has sought to combine quantitative and qualitative data, for example, by trying to measure aspects of institutional life but acknowledging the importance of meanings and definitions in determining what happens. We have taken from Harré and Secord, for example their book *An Explanation of Human Behaviour*, the prospect that qualitative methods can be subjected to the same analytic rigour as quantitative methods and contribute equally to the generation of theory.

The other research tradition influencing this study reflects attempts to chart and understand the experience of young people over time. In this, the Unit has been influenced by the work of Rutter, Quinton and colleagues on life trajectories and chains of effects. In its previous work, the Unit developed the idea of career and process and explored the ways these interact but this model has been refined in the present work by defining the terms more precisely. Life route and process are now perceived as combining to produce a career route. There has been an attempt to develop these ideas further by analysing young people's careers quantitatively, for example by identifying and measuring the effects of risk and protective factors, and qualitatively, for example, by looking at the way that young people's careers, individual circumstances and intervention experiences interact to affect outcomes. We would like to think that this approach helps take forward knowledge in this area towards better explanations of what happens to very difficult young people.

The texts that have informed the study most are as follows:

Adler, A. (1969) 'Individual psychology therapy' in Sahakian, W.(ed.), *Psycho-therapy and Counselling*, Chicago, Rand-McNally.

Ainsworth, F. (1984) 'The first 100 admissions to a regional general purpose adolescent unit', *Journal of Adolescence*, VII, 337-48.

Armstrong, H. (ed.) (1997) *Refocusing Children's Services Conference*, London, Department of Health.

Ayllon, T. and Azrin, N. (1968) *The Token Economy: A Motivational System for Therapy and Rehabilitation*, New York, Appleton-Century Crofts.

Bailey, S., Thornton, L. and Weaver, A. (1994) 'The first 100 admissions to an adolescent secure unit', *Journal of Adolescence*, XVII, 1-13.

Bailey, S. (1996) 'Adolescents who murder', *Journal of Adolescence*, XIX, 19-39.

Bailey, S. (1996b) 'Psychiatric assessment of the violent child and adolescent: Towards understanding and safe intervention' in Varma, V. (ed.) *Children and Violence*, London, Jessica Kingsley.

Bailey, S. (1997) 'Sadistic and violent acts in the young', *Child Psychology and Psychiatry Review*, II, 92-102.

Bailey, S., Kurtz, Z. and Thomes R. (1996) *A Study of the Demand and Needs for Forensic Child and Adolescent Mental Health Services in England and Wales*, London, Royal College of Psychiatrists.

Balbernie, R. (1966) *Residential Work with Children*, London, Human Context Books.

Becker, H. (1967) 'History, culture and subjective experience', *Journal of Health and Social Behaviour*, VIII, 163-76.

Becker, H. (1970) 'Problems of inference and proof in participant observation' in Filstead, W. (ed.), *Qualitative Methodology*, Chicago, Rand MacNally.

Becker, H. and Geer, B. (1967) 'Latent culture: a note on the theory of latent social roles', *Administrative Science Quarterly*, V, 304-13.

Becker, H. and Strauss, A. (1956) 'Careers, personality and adult socialization', *American Journal of Sociology*, LXII, 253-63.

Bell, L. (1997) 'The physical restraint of young people', *Child and Family Social Work*, I, 37-47.

Berry, M. (1985) *Secure Units: a Bibliography*, Special Hospitals Research Unit, University of Birmingham, 1985.

Biehal, N., Clayden, J. and Stein, M. (1995) *Moving On: Young People and Leaving Care Schemes*, London, HMSO.

Birtchnell, J. (1993) 'Does recollection of exposure to poor maternal care in childhood affect later ability to relate?', *British Journal of Psychiatry*, CLXII, 335-44.

Black, D. (1982) 'A five year follow-up of male patients discharged from Broadmoor Hospital 1960-65' in Gunn, J. and Farrington, D. (eds.), *Abnormal Offenders: Delinquency and the Criminal Justice System*, New York, Wiley.

Blau, G. and Gullota, T. (eds.) (1996) *Adolescent Dysfunctional Behaviour: Causes, Interventions and Prevention*, Thousand Oaks, Sage.

Blumenthal, G. (1985) *Development of Secure Units in Child Care*, Aldershot, Gower.

Boswell, G. (1991) *Section 53 Offenders: An Exploration of Experiences and Needs*, University of East Anglia.

Boswell, G. (1995) *Violent Victims: The Prevalence of Abuse and Loss in the Lives of Section 53 Offenders*, University of East Anglia.

Bottoms, A. and McClintock, F. (1973) *Criminals Coming of Age*, London, Heinemann.

Brown, E., Bullock, R., Hobson, C. and Little, M. (1998) *Structure and Culture in Children's Homes*, Aldershot, Ashgate.

Bullock, R., Little, M. and Millham, S. *The Characteristics of Young people in Youth Treatment Centres* (1989); *The Experiences and Careers of Young People Leaving Youth Treatment Centres* (1989); *Alternative Care Careers: The Experience of very Difficult Adolescents outside Youth Treatment Centre Provision* (1989); *The Experience of YTC Look-Alikes Sheltered in other Settings* (1994); *The Part Played by Career, Individual Circumstance and Treatment Interventions in the Outcomes of Leavers from Youth Treatment Centres (1995)*, Dartington Social Research Unit.

Bullock, R., Hosie, K., Little, M. and Millham, S. (1990), 'The characteristics of young people in Youth Treatment Centres: a study based on leavers from St. Charles and Glenthorne between 1982 and 1985', *The Journal of Forensic Psychiatry*, I, 329-50.

Bullock, R., Little, M. and Millham, S. (1983) *Residential care for Children: A Review of the Research*, London, HMSO.

Bullock, R., Little, M. and Millham, S. (1994) 'Assessing the quality of life for children in local authority care or accommodation', *Journal of Adolescence*, XVII, 29-40.

Campbell, S.B. (1990) 'Longitudinal studies of active and aggressive preschoolers: Individual differences in early behaviour and in outcome' in Cichetti, D. and Toth, S.L. (eds.), *Internalising and Externalising Expressions of Dysfunction*, Hillsdale, NJ, Erlbaum, 21-58.

Cawson, P. and Martell, M. (1979) *Children Referred to Closed Units*, London, HMSO.

Cawson, P. (1986) *Long-term Secure Accommodation: A Review of Evidence and Discussion of London's Need*, London Boroughs Children's Regional Planning Committee, 1986.

Chess, S. and Thomas, A. (1990) 'Continuities and discontinuities in temperament' in Robins, L. and Rutter, M. (eds.) *Straight and Devious Pathways from Childhood to Adulthood*, Cambridge, Cambridge University Press.

Chesson, R. and Chisholm, D. (eds.) (1995) *Child Psychiatric Units at the Crossroads*, London, Jessica Kingsley.

Cicchetti, D. (1990) 'A historical perspective on the discipline of developmental psychopathology', in Rolf, J., Masten, A., Cicchetti, D., Nuechterlein, K. and Weintraub, S. (eds.), *Risk and Protective Factors in the Development of Psycho-pathology*, Cambridge, University Press.

Clarke, A. and Clarke, A. (1984) 'Constancy and change in the growth of human characteristics', *Journal of Child Psychology and Psychiatry*, XXV, 191- 210.

Coleman, J. (1961) *The Adolescent Society*, New York, Free Press.

Cornish, D. and Clarke, R. (1975) *Residential Treatment and its Effects on Delinquency*, London, HMSO.

Cullen, E. (1994) 'Grendon: the therapeutic prison that works', *Journal of Therapeutic Communities*, XV, 301-10.

Dalton, M. (1951) 'Informal factors in career achievement', *American Journal of Sociology*, LVI, 407-15.

Dartington Social Research Unit (1995) *Matching Needs and Services: The Audit and Planning of provision for Children Looked After by Local Authorities*, Dartington.

Department of Health (annual publication) *Children Accommodated in Secure Units*, London, Government Statistical Service.

Department of Health and Social Security (1971) *Youth Treatment Centres*, London, HMSO.

Department of Health and Social Security (1979), *Report of the St. Charles Youth Treatment Centre Evaluation Team*, London.

Di Lalla, L.F. and Gottesman, I.I. (1989) 'Heterogeneity of causes for delinquency and criminality lifespan perspectives', *Developmental Psychopathology*, I, 334-49.

Ditchfield, J. and Catan, L. (1992) *Juveniles Sentenced for Serious Offences: A Comparison of Regimes in Young Offender Institutions and Local Authority Community Homes*, London, Home Office Research and Planning Unit.

Dockar Drysdale, B. (1968) *Papers on Residential Work-Therapy in Child-Care*, London, Longman.

Dolan, M., Holloway, J., Bailey, S. and Kroll, L. (1996) 'The psychosocial characteristics of juvenile sex offenders', *Medicine, Science and the Law*, XXXVI.

Dunlop, A. (1974) *The Approved School Experience*, London, HMSO.

Earls, F. (1994) 'Oppositional-defiant and conduct disorders' in Rutter, M., Hersov, L. and Taylor, E. (eds.) *Child and Adolescent Psychiatry*, Oxford, Blackwell, 308-29.

Erikson, E. (1965) *Childhood and Society*, Harmondsworth, Penguin.

Essen, J. and Wedge, P. (1982) *Continuities in Childhood Disadvantage*, London, Heinemann.

Esser, G., Schmidt, M. and Woerner, W. (1990) 'Epidemiology and psychiatric disorders in school-age children', *Journal of Child Psychiatry and Psychology*, XXXI, 243-63.

Etzioni, A. (1961) *A Comparative Analysis of Complex Organisations.* Glencoe, Free Press.

Farrington, D. (1990) 'Implications of criminal career research for the prevention of offending', *Journal of Adolescence*, XIII, 93-113.

Farrington, D. (1995) 'The challenge of teenage anti-social behaviour' in Rutter, M. (ed.), *Psychosocial Disturbances in Young People: Challenges for Prevention*, New York, Cambridge University Press.

Farrington, D. (1995) 'The development of offending and antisocial behaviour from childhood: key findings from the Cambridge Study in Delinquent Development', *Journal of Child Psychology and Psychiatry*, XXXVI, 929-64.

Farrington, D., Gallagher, B., Morley, L., St Ledger, R. and West, D. (1988) 'Are there successful men from criminogenic backgrounds?', *Psychiatry*, LI, 116-30.

Freud, A. (1946) *The Ego and the Mechanisms of Defense,* New York, International University Press.

Freud, A. (1946) *The Psycho-analytic Treatment of Children,* London, Imago.

Freud, A. (1965) *Normality and Pathology of Childhood,* New York, International University Press.

Garmezy, N. (1985) 'Stress-resistant children: The search for protective factors', *Journal of Child Psychology and Psychiatry*, IV, 213-33.

Garmezy, N. and Rutter, M. (1983) *Stress, Coping and Development in Children*, New York, McGraw-Hill.

Genders, E. and Player, E. (1995) *Grendon: A Study of a Therapeutic Prison*, London, Clarendon Press.

Godsland, J. and Fielding, N. (1985) 'Young persons convicted of grave crimes: the 1933 Children and Young Persons Act (s.53) and its effects upon children's rights', *Howard Journal of Criminal Justice*, V, 282-97.

Goffman, E. (1961) *Asylums*, New York, Anchor.

Graham, P. (1986) *Child Psychiatry: A Developmental Approach,* Oxford, Oxford Medical Publications.

Gunn, J. and Robertson, G. (1987) 'A ten year follow-up of men discharged from Grendon Prison', *Journal of Psychiatry*, CLI, 674-8.

Gunn, J., Way, C., Dell, S. and Robertson, G. (1978) *Psychiatric Aspects of Imprisonment*, London: Academic Press.

Haggerty, R., Sherrod, L., Garmezy, N. and Rutter, M. (1995) *Stress, Risk and Resilience in Children and Adolescents: Processes, Mechanisms and Interventions*, Cambridge, University Press.

Harré, R. and Secord, P. (1972), *The Explanation of Social Behaviour*, Oxford: Blackwell.

Harris, D., Cole, J. and Vipond, E. (1987) 'Residential treatment of disturbed delinquents: Descriptions of centre and identification of therapeutic factors, *Canadian Journal of Psychiatry*, 32, 579-83.

Harris, R. and Timms, N. (1993) *Secure Accommodation in Child Care: Between Hospital and Prison or Thereabouts*, London, Routledge.

Harris Hendricks, J. (1993) *When Father Kills Mother: Guiding Children through Trauma and Grief*, London, Routledge.

Heaven, P. (1996) *Adolescent Health: The Role of Individual Differences*, London, Routledge.

Heflinger, C. and Nixon, C. (eds.) (1996) *Families and the Mental Health System for Children and Adolescents: Policy, Services and Research*, Thousand Oaks, Sage.

Herbert, M. (1987) *Conduct Disorders of Childhood and Adolescence: A Formal Learning Perspective*, Chichester, Wiley.

Herbert, M. (1994) 'Behavioural methods' in Rutter, M., Hersov, L. and Taylor, E. (eds.), *Child and Adolescent Psychiatry: Modern Approaches*, Oxford, Blackwell, 858-79.

Hill, P. (1993) 'Recent advances in selected aspects of adolescent development', *Journal of Child Psychology and Psychiatry*, XXXIV, 69-100.

Hoghughi, M. (1979) 'The Aycliffe token economy', *British Journal of Criminology*, XXIX, 384-99.

Hoghughi, M. (1980) *The Aycliffe Special Unit: the First Year*, Aycliffe Studies of Problem Children.

Hoghughi, M. (1988) *Treating Problem Children*, London, Sage.

Hoghughi, M. (1992) *Assessing Child and Adolescent Disorders*, Guildford, Sage.

Hollin, C., Epps, K. and Kendrick (eds.) (1995) *Managing Behavioural Treatment: Policy and Practice with Delinquent Adolescents*, London, Routledge.

Hollin, C. and Howells, K. (1996) *Clinical Approaches to Working with Young offenders*, Chichester, Wiley.

Howells, K. and Hollin, C. (eds.) (1989) *Clinical Approaches to Violence*, Chichester, Wiley.

Izzo, R.L. and Ross, R.R.C. (1990) 'Meta-analysis of rehabilitation programmes for juvenile delinquents', *Criminal Justice and Behaviour*, 17, 134-42.

Jenkins, J. and Smith, M. (1990) 'Factors protecting children living in disharmonious homes: maternal reports,' *Journal of the American Academy of Child and Adolescent Psychiatry*, XXIX, 60-9.

Jessor, R., Donovan, J. and Costa, F. (1991) *Beyond Adolescence: Problem Behaviour and Young Adult Development*, Cambridge, University Press.

Kahan, B. (1994) *Growing Up in Groups*, London, HMSO.

Kazdin, A. (1995) *Conduct Disorders in Childhood and Adolescence*, 2nd edition., London, Sage Publications.

Kelly, B. (1992) *Children Inside: Rhetoric and Practice in a Locked Institution for Children*, London, Routledge.

Klein, M. (1932) *The Psycho-analysis of Children*, London, Hogarth.

Klein, M. (1948) *Contributions to Psycho-analysis*, London, Hogarth.

Klein, M., Heimann, P., Isaacs, S. and Riviera, J. (1952) *Developments in Psycho-analysis*, London, Hogarth.

Kolvin, I., Miller, F., Fleeting, M. and Kolvin P. (1988) 'Risk/protective factors for offending with particular reference to deprivation', in Rutter, M. (ed.), *Studies of Psycho-Social Risk: The Power of Longitudinal Data*, Cambridge, University Press, 77-95.

Labouvie, E. (1986) 'Methodological issues in the prediction of psycho-pathology' in Erlenmeyer-Kimling, L. and Miller, N. (eds.), *Lifespan Research on the Predictions of Psycho-pathology*, Hullsdale, Erlbaum, 137-55.

Lambert, R. and Millham, S. (1968) *The Hothouse Society: An Exploration of Boarding School Life through the Boys' and Girls' own Writings*, London, Weidenfeld and Nicolson.

Lambert, R., Millham, S. and Bullock, R. (1970) *A Manual to the Sociology of the School*, London, Weidenfeld and Nicolson.

Lampen J. and Neill, A. (1985) 'A bucket of cold water: a follow-up study in a residential special school', *Journal of Adolescence*, VIII, 271-88.

Lawes, E., (1979) *Role Study: St. Charles Youth Treatment Centre*, London, DHSS Social Research Branch.

Levy, A. and Kahan, B. (1991) *The Pindown Experience and the Protection of Children: The Report of the Staffordshire Child Care Inquiry 1990*, Stafford, Staffordshire County Council.

Lewin, C. and Gay, M., (1988), 'Section 53 Juvenile Offenders: Kingswood's Experience', *British Journal of Clinical and Social Psychiatry*, VI, 58-62.

Liebennan, S. (1979) *Transgenerational Family Therapy*, Guildford, Croom Helm.

Lijsel, F. and Bliesener, T. (1991) *Why do High Risk Adolescents not Develop Conduct Disorders?* Research monograph from 11th Biennial meeting of ISSBD.

Lipsey, M. (1992) 'The effects of treatment on juvenile delinquency: results from a meta-analysis' in Losel, F., Bender, D. and Bliesener, T. (eds.), *Psychology and Law: International Perspectives*, Berlin, Walter de Gruyter.

Lipsey, M.W. (1995) 'What do we learn from 400 research studies on the effectiveness of treatment with juvenile delinquents?' in McGuire, J. (ed.) *What Works: Reducing Reoffending Guidelines from Research and Practice*, Chichester, Wiley, 63-78.

Lipsey, M.W. and Wilson, D.B. (1993) 'The efficacy of psychological, educational and behavioural treatment: Confirmation from meta-analysis', *American Psychologist*, 48, 1181-209.

Little, M. (1990) *Young Men in Prison: The Criminal Identity Explored Through the Rules of Behaviour*, Aldershot, Dartmouth.

Little, M. and Kelly, S. (1995) *A Life without Problems: The Achievements of a Therapeutic Community*, Aldershot, Arena.

Loeber, R. (1990) 'Development and risk factors of juvenile antisocial behaviour and delinquency', *Clinical Psychological Revue*, 10, 1-41.

Loeber, R. and Hay, D.F. (1994) 'Developmental approaches to aggression and conduct problems' in Rutter, M. and Hay, D. (eds.) *Development Through Life: A Handbook for Clinicians*, Oxford: Blackwell Scientific.

Luthar, S. (1993) 'Methodological and conceptual issues in research on childhood resilience', *Journal of Child Psychology and Psychiatry*, XXXIV, 441-54.

Magnusson, D. and Bergman, L.R. (1990) 'A pattern approach to the study of pathways from childhood to adulthood' in Robins, L. and Rutter, M. (eds.) *Straight and Devious Pathways from Childhood to Adulthood*, Cambridge, Cambridge University Press, 101-15.

Mandel, H. (1997) *Conduct Disorder and Under Achievement: Risk Factors, Treatment and Prevention*, Chichester, Wiley.

Mannheim, H. and Wilkins, L. (1955) *Prediction Methods in Relation to Borstal Training*, London, HMSO.

Marshall, P. (1997) *A Reconviction Study of HMP Grendon Therapeutic Community*, London, Home Office Research and Statistics Directorate

Martin, D., (1977) 'Disruptive behaviour and staff attitudes at St. Charles Youth Treatment Centre', *Journal of Child Psychology and Psychiatry*, XVIII, 221-28.

McNally, R.B. (1995) 'Homicidal youth in England and Wales 1982-1992: Profile and policy', *Psychology, Crime and Law*, I, 333-42.

Millham, S., Bullock, R. and Cherrett, P. (1975) *After Grace-Teeth: A Comparative Study of the Residential Experiences of Boys in Approved Schools*, London, Human Context Books.

Millham, S., Bullock, R. and Hosie, K. (1978) *Locking Up Children: Secure Provision within the Child Care System*, Farnborough, Saxon House.

Millham, S., Bullock, R., Hosie, K. and Haak, M. (1986) *Lost in Care:. The Problems of Maintaining Links Between Children in Care and their Families*, Aldershot, Gower.

Mojena, R. (1977) 'Hierarchical grouping methods and stopping rules: an evaluation',*Computing Journal*, XX, 1977, 359-63.

Mojena, R. and Wishart, D. (1980) 'Stopping rules for Ward's clustering method', *COMPSTAT Proceedings*, Physica-Verlag, 426-32.

Morris, P. (1965) *Prisoners and their Families*, London, Allen and Unwin.

Nethercott, S. (1983) *The Aycliffe Special Unit Five Years On*, Aycliffe Studies of Problem Children.

NHS Advisory Board (1986) *Bridges Over Troubled Waters*, London.

Norris, M. (1984) *Integration of Special Hospital Patients into the Community*, Aldershot, Gower.

Oswin, M. (1978) *Children Living in Long-stay Hospitals*, London, Spastics International Medical Publication.

Parkin, W. and Green, L. (1997) 'Cultures of abuse within residential child care', *Early Child Development and Care*, CXXXIII, 73-86.

Pasamanick, B. and Knobloch, H. (1966) 'Retrospective studies on the epidemiology of reproductive causality: old and new', *Merrill-Palmer Quart*, XII, 7-26.

Petrie, C. (1980) *The Nowhere Boys*, Farnborough, Saxon House.

Petrie, C. (1986) *The Nowhere Girls*, Aldershot, Gower.

Phares, V. (1996) *Fathers and Developmental Psychopathology*, Chichester, Wiley.

Pickles, A. and Rutter, M. (1991) 'Statistical and conceptual models of turning points in developmental processes', in Magnusson, D., Bergman, G., Rudinger, G., and Torestad, B. (eds.), *Problems and Methods in Longitudinal Research*, Cambridge, University Press.

Polsky, H. (1962) *Cottage Six: The Social System of Delinquent Boys*, New York, Russell Sage.

Potter, R. (1981) 'Prediction of the need to place children in secure accommodation', *British Journal of Criminology*, XXI, 366-70.

Pyne, N., Morrison, R. and Ainsworth, P. (1985) 'A follow-up study of the first 70 admissions to a general purpose adolescent unit', *Journal of Adolescence*, VIII, 333-46.

Quinton, D., Pickles, A., Maughan, B. and Rutter, M. 'Partners, peers and pathways: assortative pairing and continuities in conduct disorder', *Development and Psychopathology*, V, 763-83.

Quinton, D. and Rutter, M. (1988) *Parenting Breakdown: The Making and Breaking of Inter-Generational Links,* Aldershot, Gower.

Robins, L. (1966) *Deviant Children Grown-up,* Baltimore, Williams and Wilkins.

Robins, L. (1991) 'Conduct disorder', *Journal of Child Psychology and Psychiatry,* XXXII, 193-212.

Rose, M. (1990) *Healing Hurt Minds,* London, Tavistock/Routledge.

Rose, M. (1997) *Transforming Hate to Love: An Outcome Study of the Peper Harow Treatment Process for Adolescents,* London: Routledge.

Rowe, J., Hundleby, M, and Garnett, L. (1989) *Child Care Now: A survey of Placement,* London, British Agencies for Adoption and Fostering.

Rutter, M. (1975) *Helping Troubled Children,* Harmondsworth, Penguin.

Rutter, M. (1978) 'Family, area and school influences in the genesis of conduct disorders' in Hersov, L., Berger, A. and Schaffer, D. (eds.), *Aggression and Anti-social Behaviour in Childhood and Adolescence,* Oxford, Pergamon.

Rutter, M. (1979) *Changing Youth in a Changing Society,* London, Nuffield Provincial Hospitals Trust.

Rutter, M. (1985) 'Psycho-pathology and development: Links between childhood and adolescent life' in Rutter, M. and Hersov, L., *Child and Adolescent Psychiatry: Modern Approaches,* Oxford, Blackwell, 720 -42.

Rutter, M. (1985) 'Psychological therapies in child psychiatry: Issues and prospects', in Rutter, M. and Hersov, L., *Child and Adolescent Psychiatry: Modern Approaches,* Oxford, Blackwell, 927-40.

Rutter, M. (1985) 'Resilience in the face of adversity: protective factors and resistance to psychiatric disorder', *British Journal of Psychiatry,* CXLVII, 598-611.

Rutter, M. (1985) 'Protective factors in children's responses to stress and disadvantage' in Kent, M. and Rolf, J. (eds.), *Primary Prevention and Psychopathology,* Hanover, VP of New England.

Rutter, M. (1988) 'Longitudinal data in the study of causal processes: some uses and pitfalls' in Rutter, M. (ed.), *Studies of Psycho-social Risk: The Power of Longitudinal Data,* Cambridge, University Press..

Rutter, M. (1989) 'Pathways from childhood to adult life', *Journal of Child Psychology and Psychiatry,* XXX, 23-52.

Rutter, M. (1994) 'Beyond longitudinal data: causes, consequences, changes and continuity', *Journal of Consulting and Clinical Psychology,* LXII, 928-40.

Rutter, M. (ed.) (1995) *Psychosocial Disturbances in Young People: Challenges for Prevention,* Cambridge, University Press.

Rutter, M. (1996) 'Developmental psychopathology: concepts and prospects' in Lenzenweger, M. and Haugaard, J. (eds.) *Frontiers of Developmental Psychopathology,* New York, Oxford University Press, 209-37.

Rutter, M. (1996) 'Transitions and turning points in developmental psychopathology: as applied to the age split between childhood and mid-adulthood', *International Journal of Behavioural Development,* XIX, 603-26.

Rutter, M., Champion, L., Quinton, D., Maughan., B. and Pickles, A. (1995) 'Understanding individual differences in environmental risk exposure' in Moen, P., Elder, H. and Luscher, K., *Examining Lives in Context: Perspectives on the Ecology of Human Development,* Washington DC, American Psychological Asssociation, pp. 61-93.

Rutter, M., Dunn, J., Plomin, R., Simonoff, E., Pickles, A., Maughan, B., Ormel, J., Meyer, J. and Eaves, L. (1997) 'Integrating nature and nurture: implications of person-environment correlations and interactions for developmental psychopathology', *Development and Psychopathology,* IX, 335-64.

Rutter, M. and Giller, H. (1983) *Juvenile Delinquency: Trends and Perspectives,* Harmondsworth, Penguin.

Rutter, M. and Gould, M. (1985) 'Classification' in Rutter, M. and Hersov, L., *Child and Adolescent Psychiatry: Modern Approaches,* Oxford, Blackwell, 304-24.

Rutter, M., Graham, P., Chadwick, O. and Yule, M. (1976) 'Adolescent turmoil: fact or fiction?', *Journal of Child Psychology and Psychiatry*, XVII, 35-56.

Rutter, M., Maughan, B., Mortimore, P., Ouston, J. and Smith, A. (1979) *Fifteen Thousand Hours*, London, Open Books.

Rutter, M. and Smith, D. (eds.) (1995) *Psychosocial Disorders in Young People: Time Trends and their Causes*, Chichester, Wiley.

Schaefer, L. and Swanson, A. (eds.) (1988) *Children in Residential Care: Critical Issues in Treatment*, New York, Van Nostrand Reinhold Company.

Sellin, T. and Wolfgang, M. (1964) *The Measurement of Delinquency*, New York, Wiley.

Shaw, R. (1987) *Children of Imprisoned Fathers*, London, Hodder and Stoughton.

Sinclair, I. (1971) *Hostels for Probationers*, London, HMSO.

Stein, M. and Carey, K. (1986) *Leaving Care*, Oxford, Blackwell.

Stewart, G. and Tutt, N. (1987) *Children in Custody*, Aldershot, Avebury.

Stewart, M., Adams, C. and Mearden, J. (1978) 'Unsocialized aggressive boys: a follow-up study', *Journal of Clinical Psychiatry*, XLIX, 797-9.

Stoney M. (1993) 'Long-term outcome in personality disorders', *British Journal of Psychiatry*, CLXII, 299-313.

Swaffer, T. and Hollin, C. (1995) 'Adolescent fire setting: why do they do it?', *Journal of Adolescence*, XVIII, 619-23.

Swaffer, T. and Hollin, C. (1997) 'Adolescents' experience of anger in a residential setting', *Journal of Adolescence*, XX, 567-76.

Tate, D., Dickon Reppucci, N. and Malvey, E. (1995) 'Violent juvenile delinquents', *American Psychologist*, L., 777-81.

Turner, T., Dossetor, D. and Bates, R. (1986) 'The early outcome of admission to an adolescent unit: a report on 100 cases', *Journal of Adolescence*, IX, 367-82.

Wadsworth, M. (1979) *Roots of Delinquency: Infancy, Adolescence and Crime*, Oxford, Martin Robertson.

Ward, J. (1963) 'Hierarchical groupings to optimise an objective formation', *Journal of American Statistical Association*, LVIII, 236-44

Wells, P. and Paragher, B. (1993) 'In-patient treatment of 165 adolescents with emotional and conduct disorders. A study of outcome', *British Journal of Psychiatry*, CLXII, 345-52..

West, D. (1982), *Delinquency: its Roots, Careers and Prospects*, London, Heinemann.

West, D. and Farrington, D. (1973) *Who Becomes Delinquent?*, London, Heinemann.

West, D. and Farrington, D. (1977) *The Delinquent Way of Life*, London, Heinemann.

Wilson, P. (1973) *Children who Kill*, London, Michael Joseph.

Wilson, P. and Hersov, L. (1985) 'Individual and group psycho-therapy' in Rutter, M. and Hersov, L., *Child and Adolescent Psychiatry: Modern Approaches*, Oxford, Blackwell, 826-38.

Winnicott, D. (1957) *The Child and the Outside World*, London, Tavistock.

Wolff, S. and Acton, W. (1968) 'Characteristics of parents of disturbed children', *British Journal of Psychiatry*, CXIV, 593-601.

Wolkind, S. and Rutter, M. (1985) 'Separation, loss and family relationships' in Rutter, M. and Hersov, L., *Child and Adolescent Psychiatry: Modern Approaches*, Oxford, Blackwell, 34-57.

Index

dartington **social research** series

This book is one of a series dealing with aspects of what is beginning to be known as a common language for the personal social services. The aims is to build up knowledge about different groups of children in need in a form that will be readily understood by policy makers, professionals, researchers and consumers and so make it possible to predict outcomes for such children and to design an effective agency response.

Secure Treatment Outcomes contributes to the enterprise in a number of ways. It predicts what happens to five groups of the most troubled children in need and shows how different sorts of intervention mediate between good and bad outcomes. It defines the concepts of **life route, process** and **career** which are key terms in the common language. It also begins to explore the connections between risk and protective factors which have the effect of moving young people between the best and the worst poles of their potential. These ideas are the focus of continuing investigation at Dartington and elsewhere.

The language of the personal social services is evolving. It is making use of the results from Dartington studies, of practical developments properly evaluated in a number of test sites and other findings from other groups working in the area. Comment from those making policy, managing services, working directly with children and families or receiving help from personal social service agencies is always welcome. There is a website describing the evolution of the common language at **www.dsru.co.uk** and a series of related papers is available from the Dartington Unit at Warren House, Warren Lane, Dartington, Totnes, Devon, TQ9 6EG email **unit@dsru.co.uk** and Fax +44-1803-866783.